RUN
SAMMY
RUN

RUN
SAMMY
RUN

Sixty-five Years
a Preacher Man

By S. S. Lappin

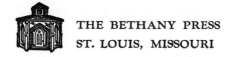
THE BETHANY PRESS
ST. LOUIS, MISSOURI

Contents

WHY THE TITLE? 7

Part I. Background

1. THE EBB TIDE OF IMMIGRATION 11
2. THE HEAD WATERS OF DRY FORK 16
3. THE LOG HOUSES OF DRY FORK 26
4. ECONOMIC PRESSURE ON DRY FORK 43
5. THE EDUCATIONAL PROCESS ON DRY FORK 53
6. THERE CAME A DAY 64

Part II. Beginnings

7. THE LITTLE TOWN OF GEFF 74
8. LITTLE TOWN CHURCHES 81
9. SCHOOL LIFE IN LITTLE TOWNS 93
10. SCHOOLS AND SCHOOLTEACHING 103
11. WORKING AND WAITING 113

Part III. Breaking Loose

12. OVER THE COUNTER 124
13. SOJOURN IN ARCADIA 137
14. LEARNING TO PREACH 145
15. COLLEGE HALLS AT LAST 160

Part IV. Learning to Read and Write

16. SOME OBSERVATIONS 173

Part V. In Retrospect

17. HIGH ESSENTIALS 187
18. LOWLY INCIDENTALS 197
19. THE WOMEN IN IT 205
20. UNFINISHED BUSINESS 216

5

Why the Title?

"Brother Lappin got pinched," said our milkman to his wife, on returning from his daily delivery route.

"So? What for?" asked the wife, surprised, and interested in all that might relate to her church and its minister.

"For speeding."

And then, quizzically, and with a half smile, the wife: "Was he driving or afoot?"

That was thought to be a justifiable joke in that community, and still is; it underlined a characteristic of mine. Of course it was a wry sort of joke to me, as I paid the required eleven dollars at the desk of the Mayor.

I have always been in a hurry. No matter where I might be going or when I am expected to arrive, I am in a hurry to get there and be done with it. The low-speed parts seem to have been out of stock when I was assembled. My mother deplored it one summer when the farmer I worked for had me following a yoke of oxen, probably the last ever used in that county or in the State of Illinois. She said it would "make me slow-motioned," so I would never be good for anything. But her fears were groundless. Released from that job and that summer on the farm, I went automatically into high and have never had any use for second speed since.

But, if you ask me, I regard it as a questionable endowment. It so often gets one into trouble. It is certain to keep him loaded down with tasks for which leisurely people have no time.

7

Besides, he will always be waiting for those of the committee who invariably come late.

In my case—and I can hear the sound of it yet—it would be "Sammy, take this letter down to the post office"; or "Sammy, run up to the grocery store and get a quarter's worth of sugar"; or when I wanted so much to sleep a little longer before sunrise, "Sammy, there's a heavy frost; you'll have to hustle out and get a hoe and cut off the sweet potato vines"; or maybe, for some neighbor, "Sammy, the Hawkins baby's got croup, run up and call the doctor"; or (when her eyesight was almost gone) "Sammy, run here and thread my needle"; or "Sammy, I've dropped a stitch in my knitting; run here and take it up for me." In any case, for one coupled up and double-charged with energy, as I have always been, it will be just another case of "Run, Sammy, Run." But it will get him somewhere—*somewhere!*

I must have been "running" true to form when I chose the text of my first sermon. I found it in John 9:4, "I must work the works of him that sent me, while it is day: the night cometh, when no man can work." Something in that text acted as a challenge to me. I think I got it across to my hearers, too, in my manner of delivery at least. I planned to make it last three quarters of an hour.

I had practiced it over and over before a timepiece, but to the surprise of my listeners, and to my own chagrin, I got through in fifteen minutes. I have thought some of going back to that country schoolhouse to deliver a discourse to the third generation of my first auditors, just to prove that now, when threescore years have flown, I can preach longer than fifteen minutes. But I have never had time for it. Anyway, fifteen minutes is all the public will stand for, or sit for, now; so perhaps I would do better to pose as the farseeing pulpiteer who, so long ago, even in his youth, saw what was coming and set the pace.

Again, and significantly, in the first year of my settled ministry I perpetrated a bit of rhymed composition expressive of that questionable and often-embarrassing trait of mine. Presuming on the patience and long-suffering of my readers I dare to submit here, as further excuse for the unconventional title of this book, that unpretentious metrical effusion:

If all my castles built in bygone years,
Vain plans, lost joys and needless fears,
And all my verdant hopes were brought today,
And laid before me in diverse array,
'Twould only prompt within, the thought sublime,
The importance of the present time.

If all the valued friends of long ago,
Whose voices and whose forms I used to know,
And all the dear, sweet memories of the past,
Were in one panoramic vision cast,
And all could greet my wondering gaze,
Of even greater worth I'd hold these passing days.

If all my work, unfinished, left behind,
If all my doings, the helpful, the unkind,
With all my doubts and failures and my sins
Were shown to me as each new day begins,
I could but take the moments one by one,
And gild the present with some task well done.

If all that future decades hold in store,
Of griefs and joys, of troubles deep and sore;
If all the saddening changes I shall see,
Should be, from now henceforth, well known to me,
I could make no other, better vow
Than to build the future from the now.

Enough by way of introduction—and apology—for the title and the contents of this book. There are other and better ways than that herein described. But it was so, in my case, that I could not choose a way—I had to make a way; and I must lose no time getting about it. And now that the eventful journey down the years may be drawing to a close, I must say, with such wisdom as comes from experience, that I do not see how, for me, it could have been much different. I do not commend to others the road I have had to travel or the rate of speed kept up through threescore years and ten. These are only for such as are nerved and driven as I was, by an insistent desire to know and do and be.

For any who are thus inspired and inhibited, I give due warning. There are rough roads that way, with hurdles and handicaps innumerable. But I bear glad witness to any who may come after that the route, however difficult and delaying, gives promise of abundant reward at last. I can say this of it, no matter what the toils of the road have been, it brought me, hop, skip, and jump, by experimental shortcuts and many a delaying detour from one of the thousand hardscrabbles in America, located in a sordid rural slum on Dry Fork in Southern Illinois, to a conspicuous pulpit in the university area of Pittsburgh. That, too, with only a scant eighth-grade formal schooling and without pull or bull or any of the aids commonly supposed to be essential, if not indispensable, to professional attainment with no assistance save the kindly encouragement of generous friends along the way.

That interesting and eventful journey of a lifetime is what this book is about. The road traveled is still open. It may have been improved somewhat in these later days; indeed I think it has. But it is not, and never will be, an easy road to travel. Let any try it who will—or who must.

S. S. Lappin, Minister at Large,
Redbud Bungalow, Bedford, Ind.

10

PART I. Background

Chapter 1

The Ebb Tide of Immigration

The road-weary team of mustangs and the dust-covered, ramshackle wagon turned into a little lane with persimmon trees along one side. The outfit drew up and came to a standstill on the chipyard under a honey locust tree in front of a comfortable farmhouse of hewed logs.

We were at Uncle David's. The slow, sorrowful journey over four hundred miles of primitive roads was ended at last, and that new-made grave, a yellow ridge on a briar-grown hillside, full two hundred miles away.

A plump, good-natured woman came out to scold her recently bereaved sister, Jane, coaxingly, and to pat each dark head of the three youngsters that climbed stiffly down from the wagon. A tall, spare, leathery-faced man came in from the fields for a glimpse of such a batch of flotsam as is seldom cast up by the social and economic tides of a troubled world. It was the wreckage of an ignominious emigrant experience

11

brought back by the ebb tide, like driftwood, and laid at the door of a southern Illinois farmer.

Uncle David was a poor man, though he owned a farm. But he seemed rich to us, homeless in that covered wagon for weeks, if only because he had a house to live in. But if he was a poor man, as judged by the intrinsic value of things owned, he was none the less a man; and such a one as may be met but a half dozen times in threescore years and ten. Politically a Democrat; fraternally a Freemason; religiously a Universalist, he was at the same time a common court of appeal for farm families over a wide circuit.

Uncle David, in the greatness of his heart, took us in and shared with us the simple comforts of his humble home.

Just why Joe Lappin ever took Jane Strahl Lappin and their small children into the Ozarks and to the particular spot he chose, I have never been quite able to figure out. He was seeking a home for us, of course; and it may have been that the low wooded hills of Monroe County, Ohio, or the plentiful firewood he had been used to in Illinois had intrigued him. More probably, I think, it was an unconscious desire to get away from the crowd, to find solitude, to end the homeless wanderings bred in him by two centuries of Huguenot ancestry.

He was the son of Knight Lappin. Knight was son of Robert, Irish refugee of Revolutionary times. Robert had married Elizabeth Kirk, daughter of Joseph. Kirk had married Judith Knight in the old Quaker meetinghouse at East Nottingham, in what was then Maryland—later Pennsylvania. The names Joseph and Knight and Kirk followed down the line.

Joseph Kirk, with his son-in-law, Robert Lappin, moved to Fayette County, Pennsylvania, from which location, according to records in Uniontown Courthouse, Robert enlisted in the War of 1812. Then, following recurrent waves of immigration, the family drifted westward. Robert stopped in Ohio and died there—in Vinton County, though he had lived in Monroe.

12

Of his three sons, Robinson and Knight moved to Wayne County, Illinois, and Samuel to Iowa. In 1878 Robinson's family moved to Phillips County, Kansas. Knight's family divided; two, William and George, remained in Illinois, merchandising at Xenia for many years; and Jonathan and Joe took to the road again in 1870 to Southwestern Missouri. The story of one family is the story of a thousand in that time when our American population was aswarm.

There must have come to be an incurable migrant tendency in the sons of the Huguenot dispersion. They went into all the countries of Europe, more than three hundred thousand of them. Some remained where they first settled. Many but paused and then sought more satisfactory contacts under some other flag. Very many fled at once to America for the new life they were to live. There is a settlement of Lappins in Grodna, Russia—all of them Jews. Another numerous company of the name were mingled with the French weavers who settled about Lisburn, Ireland, after the Battle of the Boyne. A numerous company sought refuge and freedom in the then new world.

Many Huguenot families in Great Britain changed their names when Napoleon was trying to get across the channel. Leblanc became White; Lenoir became Black; Leroy became King; Le Tonnellier became Cooper; Lappin was not changed —it would have been rabbit if it had been anglicized. The American Lappins came mostly from the Lisburn colony. Robert, my great-grandfather, sang Irish songs in a German brogue and used to tell his grandchildren how he was born on the sea, the son of a Huguenot refugee and an Irish gentlewoman who left her home to marry him. Most of the Lappins in this country are Protestant, but some of the original stock are Roman Catholic; a good many are unbranded mavericks. In every individual I have sounded there is a deep strain of somber sentiment verging on the melancholy.

13

His brother George, contemporary with Lincoln, loved the favorite poem of the President under whom he served in the Civil War, "Oh, why should the spirit of mortal be proud?" I never knew a man of the name who did not like to walk in the woods and watch the trees as the wind roared through them on a stormy day in winter. I, myself, have had always to lean away from the morbid, depressing things of life. I could easily compose a book of lamentations. But I would not be the better for doing so, nor would anyone else; and I would miss a lot of fun. I whistle a good deal to keep from whining; one can't do the two things at the same time.

Six years in the gumbo hills of Missouri, two of schoolteaching in Bolivar, and four in a fight with stump and stone, were enough for Joe Lappin. He had married Jane Strahl in Illinois and they had three children. He had never been a robust man. He had failed to pass for service in the Civil War. Pneumonia in his youth had weakened him.

One night as he was falling asleep, his throat filled with a warm fluid, and he arose to empty his mouth into his palm at the moonlit doorway of their cabin home. It was blood, bright arterial blood. No diagnosis was needed then to explain what that meant; it was a death sentence, the event not long deferred.

Equity on a half-cleared farm was exchanged for a team of mules, the family effects loaded into a covered wagon and a trek of four hundred miles begun back to the old home country, Southern Illinois, where relatives on both sides still lived.

The trip was calculated to take four weeks if no delays occurred. At Springfield the mules that had been found to be but half broke were traded for a team of mustang ponies. Then, after consultation with a rather noted local physician, who spoke no hopeful word, Jane Lappin with her sick husband and their three young children began the long, desolate transit over hill and vale with no knowledge of the route or, more important, of the future that lay beyond at the journey's end.

14

On May 8, 1877, Joe Lappin died in a roadside cabin, a primitive meetinghouse, with only his little family present. The wagon had broken down on a hilly road near Crocker, Missouri. When he knew the end was near, he looked up with tired eyes into Jane's face and said, "Oh, Jane, I've got to die and leave you and the children here among strangers." He exacted from her that night the promise that she would continue to the end of the journey as planned. She kept the promise. Of the seven dollars left her then, she had five at her journey's end. So it was that the four of us came to pause that day among relatives on the southern Illinois farm of my Uncle David Truax.

On July 20 of that same year, my mother gave birth to twin sons, increasing her dependent ones to five! Her eyesight had begun to dim at fifteen. She was half blind now, never able to see one of her children clearly enough to recognize him. No more pitiful case of utter destitution have I ever known. I was seven then—too young to sense it all, as I now do.

Our mother, in childbed with a boy baby on each arm, looked up into the face of the attending physician and said, "It would seem to me that of all the things on earth that I do not need, a pair of twins would take first place." That good man smiled and said, with some show of emotion, "You can't ever tell about such things, Mrs. Lappin; these boys may prove to be a gift of God to you; we'll have to wait and see." Just that, presently, they proved to be.

Chapter 2

The Head Waters of Dry Fork

We were to be at home on the terrain of a creek known locally as "Dry Fork," whose sluggish waters found their way, by many windings and through larger streams, to the Gulf of Mexico. There are hundreds of dry forks in this vast land of ours, no doubt, and thousands of families destitute and distressed. But out of such surroundings, through human initiative and the providence of God, flow, presently, the "streams of influence that enrich the conscience of the world." Dry Fork—I despise the very name because of the sordidness and spiritual poverty it suggests; to another it might have happiest associations.

In the log house that we lived in, as I well remember, were two cord beds; an old, worn-out cookstove; four chairs; a wide rocker we called the ferry boat; and some sort of cupboard. These discarded things were donated by kindly neighbors a little better off than were we. In a nearly roofless barn were two ponies. A farmer had contributed a double-shovel plow and a harrow of primitive pattern. A great-aunt (wife of Robinson) gave us a cow that we called "Old Cherry." With these we somehow got through the first summer. When winter came, one of the ponies, the nervous fiery one of which we were all

16

afraid, had to go. The fifty dollars he brought supplied clothes for all of us and schoolbooks for the two older children.

Though past seven, I stayed at home that winter. My daily task was to gather wood from the nearby forest for fireplace and cookstove; when this was done, I read to my mother out of an old hymnbook. The metrical arrangement of words between the musical scores stumped me and she could not see to give direction, but a kindly neighbor helped us out. Mother memorized the words and, remembering the tunes she had learned on Sunday Creek in Ohio, she made the forest ring as she went about her housework. Thus she assuaged her grief and healed the hurt her soul had suffered.

In gathering wood I had to go farther and farther each day to find in the dead tops of felled trees the brittle limbs I could break up into fit lengths. Often I lost my direction and might have had difficulty getting back but for her singing. I was never so far from the fireside that I could not hear the strains of her favorite hymn:

> Where no storms ever beat on that glittering strand
> And the years of eternity roll . . .

Her second favorite hymn was "The Sunbright Clime." It began with these lines:

> Say, friends, have you heard of that sunbright clime,
> Undimmed by sorrow, unhurt by time
> Where age ne'er dims the fadeless frame,
> Where the eye is fire and the heart is flame . . .
> Have you heard of that sunbright clime?

Next in preference was one that, for lack of any other title, one of the twins presently came to call "Beauty." Rocking to and fro in the old armchair in Mother's arms, one would say,

17

"Sing 'Beauty,' Ma, sing 'Beauty,'" and her strong, clear voice would ring out with,

> You may sing of the beauty of mountain and dale,
> Of the silvery streamlet and flowers of the vale;
> But the place most delightful this earth can afford,
> Is the place of devotion, the house of the Lord.

There was no "house of the Lord" anywhere near to which she could go. The two men in that region who could have been instrumental in forming a church and in safeguarding the moral values of the neighborhood were William Slack and David Truax; and both men claimed to be Universalists. That claim was but an alibi, as it usually is—a flight from the reality of sin, an opiate for the conscience that cries out in protest against godless living.

At the root of all our community's weakness and wickedness, as I now know, was this: that we had no church, no religious life, no Lord's day. A large proportion of the outlawry, scandal, crime, and litigation that came into the county court came from Dry Fork. Young married folk of highly respectable families took up residence there only to lose the good qualities bred and trained into them elsewhere. Families or members of families moving out, and to within radius of religious organization and influence, rose quickly to higher levels of social life.

Three times, and only three, in that bitter, blighting six years did my mother get us to religious services. Once we went to Dry Fork schoolhouse where a tiresome, droning old egotist spent an hour trying to show a handful of yokels how much he knew. My mother would not go there again.

Once we went six miles in a neighbor's farm wagon to Pleasant Grove church where we attended Sunday services in the forenoon and at night. At the close of the evening service I awoke lying flat on my back on a front seat and saw a man

18

with a scant black mustache walking back and forth above me crying out, "The Spirit and the bride say, 'Come,' let him that heareth say, 'Come,' and whosoever will, let him take of the water of life freely." I did not know at all what it meant until years afterward when I heard him speak the words in invitation again and again.

Once we three children attended Sunday school at Oak Valley Baptist church within long walking distance of one of the log houses we occupied. I had no shoes as did the other boys in my class and tried to hide my bare feet by thrusting them back under the seat. When we got home my older brother told our mother, with some show of pride, "Sam was the smallest boy in the class but he could read better and answer more questions than any of the rest."

The service that took deepest hold on me was a meeting for communion in the home of Uncle Billy Wilson. There was reading of the Bible, a prayer, a song or two, and then with solemnity, a "stand table" on which was a glass plate, a little cake of bread, and a goblet with some red fluid was uncovered. Uncle Jimmy Sons prayed, and with his big brown hands, handled the "emblems"; two other men waited on those present. I watched to see if my mother would partake, and she did. I wondered if they would pass the plate and cup to me, and they did not. Riding home on horseback behind my mother, I asked her what it meant and in one sentence she delivered the most effective communion sermon I have ever heard. She said, in a subdued and reverential tone, "We do that in memory of Jesus, our Savior, who died for us and is now in heaven where we all hope to go sometime." That half-blind and hopelessly marooned mother of mine was deeply religious and hungry in heart always for spiritual food. She would have attended religious services regularly but could not; she was far ahead of many more fortunate ones who could but would not.

19

What type of social life could be expected where light shone so seldom and so dimly among the people? Our spiritual poverty harbored a foul brood of moral delinquencies among merry-hearted, growing young people.

Each neighborhood has its gang of boys. Among the older ones will be a leader admired by the others. Around him will be gathered his cabinet of near great ones. On the fringe of the group will be younger boys hearing all and wishing they could have larger part in it. I was of this outer group in the Dry Fork gang, a sort of mascot, a runt, really.

Most of the talk of the older ones, both up the creek and down, had to do with savage fights and exploits with women and girls—proofs, as all thought, of mature manliness. On our Sunday tours of wood and stream, little attention was paid to fishing, hunting, birdnesting and other such wholesome activities. We might climb a mulberry tree in season, or gather hazelnuts and pawpaws, enough to satisfy hunger. Or we might make stealthy raids on orchard or melon patch. We always went swimming when the water was not too cold; that somehow fitted in with the main theme. Bare human bodies are suggestive of strength and virility.

What should have been to us a training period was a season of mental and moral debauchery. I was youngest of the group and a listener only, but an admirer in boyish way, of most that the older ones said and did.

There was not, I now believe, a bad boy in that crowd. They but fell in with such amusement and youthful pastime as was afforded in that community during their hours of leisure. Although our group indulged in all the practices frowned upon and condemned by older people, no kindly older person ever counseled one of us as to the evil of it and no group of men and women ever banded together in a Sunday school to entice us into better ways. The hurt to most of us was not early decline, insanity, and the dire consequences described in the printed advertisements of quacks and charlatans such as fell into the hands of us all. Perhaps the literature we read did us more harm in the fears and misgivings awakened than did the sordid practices the gray-bearded old doctors so deplored and vainly sought to check by the nostrums they had to sell. Looking back at the group it seems to me now that the chief hurt was in lowered idealism, an unholy and unwholesome attitude toward womanhood, and the drift of some into an utterly foul mentality. I somehow got away from all that; it was my first and longest step toward decency and self-respect.

Sunday afternoon was my worst time. Usually the gang straggled back from the woods by one o'clock. Then we broke up into twos and threes and scattered to our homes for the late Sunday dinner then common. My older brother usually went away with other boys of his own age. My mother and sister, with the twins, would be at home or visiting some neighbor. I would be left alone.

I would go back to the woods, to some different tract or spot to find such amusement as I might. And always, for no reason that I then knew or can now imagine, I would be overcome with a spasm of weeping, an outburst of emotion I did not understand. Such loneliness, such dejection, such abject, unutterable misery. Many a time in happier days that came presently, the dreams of nighttime have borne me back and I have wandered in deep, tangled brushwood, among the fallen trees, and along dry creek beds alone, disconsolate, uncomforted, crying, crying, crying, until by exertion of will I roused myself from what I knew, even in sleep, was but a dream. It has taken the long processes of the years between to remedy this deep-planted melancholy. I learned to find companionship and comfort in helping others.

We lived four miles from the town of Jeffersonville, later called Geff. The town consisted of twoscore houses, four small stores, two churches, and a schoolhouse, built on a sector of

21

the O. & M. Railroad, afterward the B. & O. That distance we walked often, for such necessities as soda, salt, coffee, sugar, and rice. When Old Charley, our one horse, was not at work in the field, or when grist had to be taken to mill, I might ride in on horseback without saddle. Once I made the journey on foot to get ten cents' worth of soda and three cents' worth of fishhooks. In the excitement of selecting and admiring my fishhooks, I forgot the soda and had to go back next day to get it. Another time I took that long trudge over snowy roads in winter to get vaccinated, and found myself waterbound by quick-melting snow. I had to wade the icy water of Martin Creek waist-deep to get home. For that I should have died of pneumonia, I suppose, but it did not affect me in the least. I have waded in snow in bare feet every winter since, just for the fun of it.

I did not like the town boys. They always bullied me. Though they seemed fierce, I knew that back of it all was but the childish wish of the boy to seem brave to a stranger. I did not resent their threatenings, for I was one and they several; in a scrimmage they might gang up on me.

Once my sister and I had to go to town on an errand for our mother. We were not hurried that day and took time to explore the several streets. It was near holiday time and the Christmas wares were on display in the store windows, unbelievably attractive to the hungry eyes of rural children. We loitered about the stores, begged for almanacs and empty boxes; we admired the frame houses, so neat and white they seemed; we enjoyed the board sidewalks and followed each one of them to its end, passing the two churches, the mill with its great pond, the mammoth schoolhouse of three rooms with its bell on a tall framework outside. On our way out of the village we spied half a dozen bright empty oyster cans under the edge of a building. We gathered them eagerly; we could use them in our playhouse down by the branch. Then, as we came near the depot, we met a swaggering youth, the postmaster's son, who accosted us banteringly as he spied the cans we would have been glad to hide but could not now cast away. "Ho, ho, goin' to have some soup, I see." He was making fun of us and we knew it. We were to know Nate Ulm better later on.

I walked to Geff once, late in autumn, with a lady who asked me to go with her "just for company." We went into all four of the stores that day and lingered in each one for a time. Again it was nearing the holiday season. While my companion did her trading, I took account of everything in sight. It was all wonderful to me. I walked home empty-handed. That night I was tired and sore at heart. Before I slept, I looked back over it all with a clear conviction that injustice had someway been done me. I blamed no one. I was just a poor, helpless, orphaned boy. I was crying silently before I slept. My mother, always watchful of our moods and deeply sensitive to any hurt we might suffer, heard my tremulous breathing and asked the cause of my grief. I told her that it was because I had to go to town and see all the pretty things and could not buy any of them. She drew me to her, wrapped me in her arms, sobbed with me until I was awed by her grief and forgot my own. And then, as she held me close, she rehearsed the misfortunes we had suffered and said, "It will not always be like this; we will not always be so poor; some day you can earn money and buy things like other boys." Then I tried to comfort her by saying that I would buy things for her too. That night came the first intense cold of winter. Before I slept, I heard the roof timbers of the old house pop and crack as frost contracted them. But next morning I was up early digging in the ashes of the fireplace for the few coals I could find and gathering bits of dry bark to strew over them for the beginning of a fire. "Sufficient unto the day is the evil thereof." "Weeping may endure for a night but joy cometh in the morning." We would not always be poor!

23

My heart sang all day—I had a secret—someday I would earn money and buy things—things for my mother!

The main highway of our neighborhood was known as the Wilson and Tunnel Road. The older route, known as the Vandalia Trace, which led from Grayville to Vandalia, the first state capital, had crossed our Big Road not far from Hardscrabble School. I used to wonder why ours was named for Wilson and Tunnel but have never taken pains to find out. I wondered, too, where it led beyond the schoolhouse to the north and beyond Covington to the south. I knew only that the road paralleled Dry Fork as nearly as a measurably straight road can parallel a miserably crooked stream.

There were ghosts in that day. We heard about them frequently. Sometimes we thought we had seen one. The stories we heard and told were the real thing. That they lost nothing in the retelling I can now be sure. As to the ghosts themselves, a wider acquaintance with the universe outside of Dry Fork neighborhood has raised some doubts as to just what it was we saw.

A favorite fireside narrative, one of the most fearsome ones to children, had to do with one Doctor Shirley and his ride home from a deathbed one night. The story declared that as he rode along on horseback under trees that overhung from either side, the Doctor heard singing. It would be in the air above him, or under his horse, or in the bushes at either side. Hymn tunes were the staple of this strange nightly companion of the journeying physician. If he sang with the ghost, it would ring out louder with wailing tones, but if he hummed or whistled a "dancing tune," the ghost instantly let up. I can imagine that his horse went loping home to the tune of "Old Dan Tucker," though there is no evidence to that effect. The story lacked a climax either of terror or disillusionment. But no lone urchin, such as I, ever went along the Wilson and Tunnel Road, even in daytime, that he did not start with a shiver of fear and maybe

24

run in terror down the road at the slightest unusual noise among the trees. It ought to be added, perhaps, that Doctor Shirley was said to make use of drugs or stimulants on occasion when his physical strength lagged under unusual strain.

This particular story played a part in an amusing little drama. Two youths were returning from Covington amid the gathering shadows one evening. One of them had been regaling his visiting cousin with this Doctor Shirley legend. The guest was plainly skeptical, besides he was known never to be scared at anything. He chuckled over it as they were picking their way among brushpiles in a clearing on a short cut toward home.

"You say it stopped when he whistled a dancing tune?"

"Yes, every time."

"That seems queer," said the skeptical one. "I reckon that ghost had been attending a revival meeting somewhere."

"Dunno," answered his companion, and they were having trouble finding their way in the deepening darkness.

Suddenly an old fox hound, treading soft grass out of sight and all unknown to the boys, let off such a wild quavering wail as only a hound can utter.

Instantly the unbelieving guest struck an attitude of abject terror and began whistling in a loud high key, "The Arkansas Traveler." That convulsed both boys and felled the ghost.

No doubt, there were many rural scenes not unlike that I have described. There may be some yet in remote regions. I can recall Frog Island, Hickory Hill, Barefoot Nation, and Brush Creek, and the echoes of strifes and scandals that came to our ears concerning these parts.

Many things that begin on Dry Fork are not finished there; and many that begin there are never finished.

Chapter 3

The Log Houses of Dry Fork

Most of the log houses of the first settlers were standing when we arrived on Dry Fork. Some of them had been enlarged by an added frame structure or lean-to and others had been moved back and displaced by more pretentious residences. We seem to have lived in all of the unoccupied ones at one time or another. There were, successively, the Aunt Betsy Windland place, the Worstenholm place, the Handsacker place, the Tom Finty cabin, the Tom Finty house—four rough walls, always, and an indifferent roof with floor of rough boards. But they were rent-free to us, as I remember, all of them—we were to tend a few acres "on the shares."

Families went visiting at night. Once or twice neighbors came to our place. More often our mother, in the sheer desperation that is sometimes born of loneliness, took us to visit in some larger and more comfortable home. On such occasions there were three major amusements. There would be riddles: "big at the bottom, little at the top, something in the middle goes whippity-whop." The answer, of course, is a churn. This one and others like it were the old regulars; occasionally someone had a new one. There might be stories, usually fearsome ones that would make me hold my mother's hand tightly as we walked home. Songs were popular and were usually ancient religious refrains: "I'm on my way to Canaan [pronounced Canyan usually], I'm on my way to Canaan, I'm on my way to Canaan, the fair and happy land"; then "Oh brothers, will you meet me . . ." "Oh sisters, will you meet me . . ." and "Oh fathers, will you meet me . . .," and so on through the whole list of kinsfolk, until finally "Oh neighbors, will you meet me." This was absolute intellectual relaxation with never a word to instruct, to edify, to inform, or to elevate, yet it was a fantastic flight from grim reality.

At our occasional family gatherings we might have refreshments—but also, we might not. The staple would be parched field corn done to brown brittleness in a skillet, a meat skin thrown in to grease it as the grains swelled with heat. Popcorn had not been discovered yet, I think; at least we had never heard of it. There might be an "apple hole" in the garden; but more likely our fruit course would be a turnip. Sometimes hickory nuts or hazelnuts were in evidence.

Sunday visiting was common. To go someplace for dinner, or to have someone come, was a break in the tedium of dragging days. Gossip that shaded off into scandal was of constant occurrence. The private talk of women was matched only by the obscenity and profanity of men and boys. Perhaps the slight scandals each day kept the big scandals away. For there was, withal, a willingness to help in time of need. Neighbors who picked each other to pieces socially might, on occasion, patch each other up physically if sickness or accident came.

Aunt Nancy Windland used to come over to the Tom Finty house occasionally in cool weather to visit with my mother and talk the afternoon away by the open fire. They had known each other in earlier life so that neighborly relations were natural enough.

Aunt Nancy and Uncle Jackson lived some fifty rods west of the creek and we as far east. With no public meetings, no news-

27

papers, no telephones and with only wagon paths for roads, deep with dust or mud when not hard and knobby from freezing, there was something of luxury in the occasional call of a neighbor. Even I, a boy of eleven and always busy with wood-getting or trapping or whittling, invariably knocked off for the afternoon when Aunt Nancy came.

Watching the two of them before the radiant fireplace, elbows on knees, gossiping, I used to wish there were something a boy could do that would let him in on that fellowship and give him the satisfaction that seemed to be theirs.

I enjoyed the gossip of the neighborhood as well as did they. But sometimes my mother would turn kindly to me and send me on some errand improvised at the moment, as I could see, and usually at the most interesting place in the conversation. I knew, of course, that they were going to talk about things they did not wish a boy to hear. I always went without protest but I never failed to hurry back. Usually, though, I came within hearing distance too late to get more than the general drift of what had been said in my absence. What little I did hear, pieced together by a boy's imagination, convinced me that there were things of interest to a boy of my age that I was not supposed to know about. Thus stimulated, and with the aid of other boys, an older brother among them, I proceeded speedily to inform myself concerning such matters. It would have been altogether better for them and for me if I had heard all the two of them had to say. Placing the cookie jar on the top shelf saves no cookies, but it trains the boy to climb.

One oft-repeated item of these afternoon reviews never escaped me. My mother, still lamenting the loss of her companion, would usually get round to the mention of her bereavement. And Aunt Nancy, pointing with her right forefinger at me, the sole and silent listener to their talk, would say, solemnly, "And Jane, there's a boy that'll go just like his father."

I supposed that Aunt Nancy knew; at least it never occurred to me at the time to doubt her assertion. But the thirty years between eleven and forty-one, at which age my father had died, seemed to me quite satisfactory, so I let it pass at that.

Dear old Aunt Nancy, unlettered, unreligious, unmoral, unknown to the world, and unsung when her humble life went out! Many's the piece of bread and butter and jelly she gave a hungry boy—wheat bread, too, it was, in contrast with ours that was so often of cornmeal or "shorts." She was untaught in the ways of the world but she knew the things necessary to the life she lived. Risqué as was much of her gossipy conversation, it was wholesomely so, less harmful and far less dangerous than much to be seen in the movies, read in the magazines, or carried on in high school atmosphere today. And who can say what good may have resulted among the straying sons and daughters of men by nagging tongues like hers, keeping them, through fear of exposure, to the straight and narrow way? There seems to me now to have been something roughly and uncouthly American about what went on at the fireplace. The two women were but having their say about matters in general. That very thing, harnessed, implemented, and wrought into intelligent self-expression, is what we call the democratic process.

My mother was not like Aunt Nancy, friends though they were. Her mind moved at different tempo and, normally, on a higher level; she thought of other things than local contacts could suggest; much that went on about her called for tolerance; some of it was charitably covered by her sense of humor. She was the mother and protector of an orphaned brood. She must supply food; she must exercise oversight; she and she alone was responsible for the future of the five of us without money or influential friends. Aunt Nancy was a sort of refuge and relaxation for her, a buffer to take up the shock of collision with unavoidable hardship. Their neighborly speech together always left my mother in more courageous mood.

But I had to disappoint Aunt Nancy; though I remember her awesome prediction with deep gratitude, it proved but a challenge. On Wash Branch, without argument to offer in rebuttal, I was willing to admit that she might be right in her confident forecast of an untimely end for me; it seemed a long way off and there was nothing I could do about it anyway. I had my fishing in summer and my trapping in winter, and always my whittling.

One day I somehow got hold of a copy of McLean's Almanac and read it from cover to cover, as I usually did every line of print that came my way. Old Doctor McLean submitted, along with testimonials for his medicines, several pages of sensible health talk. There I read that if every person would breathe deeply ten times in succession and a dozen times a day, pulmonary tuberculosis could be eradicated in a generation. By that time life had begun to take on a certain lustre. I decided that I would not mind living beyond forty-one. So, since the prescription of Doctor McLean was free and the ingredients abundant and close at hand, I decided to try it. And try it I did, and have to this day, with persistence and regularity.

At twenty-three, I applied for my first life insurance and the examiner shook his head doubtfully as he inquired into my family history. "Consumption, eh?" he muttered as he filled in the blank. But when he came to take my chest measurement, he seemed mystified and measured me twice, urging complete deflation and inflation. Then he gave a low whistle of amazement, "Five and a half inches chest expansion—and for a man of your height and weight! How come?" I told him about Aunt Nancy's dire prediction, and he smiled; then I told him about Doctor McLean's counsel, and he frowned. I think he would have been better pleased had I died according to Aunt Nancy than to have had me live and thrive under the advice of a vendor of patent medicines. Thanks to Aunt Nancy and old Doctor McLean I am my own physician, in the main, as I am my own theologian. I have had observation of this body and spirit more constantly and for a longer time than has anyone else; all curative agents are accessible to me and I am in possession of all the revelations God has ever made to mankind.

We had some benefit from living in log houses. There was no lack of ventilation. Constant exposure to chill atmospheres and a scant diet of plainest foods kept colds away. We were not exposed to sweets and fats or excess of meats and starchy foods that encourage constipation, the forerunner or attendant of nearly every chronic disease.

Of course, everyone had ague. We did not know how serious malaria was and therefore did not die of it. Nobody knew what caused it. Some laid it to "dog days" when scum formed on pools in the streams and when boys must not go swimming. We were nearer the truth than we knew. We had our home remedies—boneset, blackroot, lobelia, and the staple drug remedy, quinine. All medicines given for ague were bitter—the more bitter the better. But the worst decoction of them all was a tea of boneset and blackroot combined. My mother had great confidence in this; it gagged us so. But in spite of them all I had "third-day ague" for a solid year, terminating with a summer of colic which made my life one of long-drawn-out misery. However, few families of six ever got by with as little physical discomfort or as few doctor's bills.

One case of serious illness occurred, however. I was the victim. My ailment, typhoid pneumonia, came upon me as suddenly as a stroke of apoplexy. My mother was giving me a bath in the wash tub when I cried out with sudden and unendurable pain. She hurried me to bed and sent for Doctor Barrackman. When consciousness returned six weeks later, I had but one memory of the interim. Over and over I had escaped from the watchers and run down the woodsy path to a wet-weather spring where we got water and had lain down and drunk it dry so that I had to wait for it to fill up before I could

31

drink again. Then, in an instant, I was in bed with the old thirst burning me up. The technique of the time forbade water to fever patients. I lived through that torment, for a wonder; and Doctor Barrackman lived to treat my two brothers to ice water and ice cream when, at sixteen, they suffered from typhoid.

Our lesser ills were treated by my mother. Her favorite remedies were soda, sulphur, hickory bark tea, hot baths, and decoctions made from the herbs we gathered in the fall. Her favorite resource, next to soda, was lobelia. Both were emetics, soda mildly so. I was alkaline already and did not need it. But lobelia would empty the stomach in a minute. Enough lobelia to produce thorough vomiting followed by enough soda to act as a cathartic was her technique; and, distasteful as it was, it did more to relieve acute illnesses than many a course of treatment I have taken that was twice as complicated and ten times as costly.

It was not easy to keep warm in the log houses. Neither stove nor fireplace would do more than heat up a local zone in the frigid atmosphere when the mercury went down, down, down, to ten or twenty below, as it sometimes did. We had no lack of fuel. Timber was plentiful and nearby. Every winter neighbor men came for a woodchopping. Their axes rang all about, and that pile of logs and limbs mounted until it seemed to me I never would be able to cut it all up into usable lengths. That was my responsibility, and the ax was always dull.

We had an old shovel we used for the fireplace. When removing hot ashes from under the forestick, the handle of the shovel would get hot and sometimes break into a blaze. That meant that a new handle had to be made occasionally. I took great pride in my new shovel handles and my mother never failed to praise me when I brought one in. I would find a hickory of the right size, hack it down with our old ax, cut it to the right length and remove the bark. Then I would drive it into the neck of the shovel and fasten it with a nail broken off of some timber in the barn. When it was finished and ready for use, I would bring it in, stand it up by the jamb, and call my mother's attention to it. She would run her hands over it and speak her never-failing word of appreciation. I would sit and look at that new shovel handle and wish we could have everything in the house new like that. I resolved that we should someday. I thought it would be a help toward better things. It has been.

The food problem was always difficult. Mother managed that somehow. One winter it was the surprising patch of late potatoes that brought us through—Iowa Reds, they were, and delicious to the hungry palate no matter how they were cooked. We usually raised enough corn for Old Charley and to fatten a pig. What a relish we had for fresh meat when butchering day came! For one period of six months—in the Bad Year (1880)—we tasted no crumb of wheat bread. Then a kind neighbor brought us a loaf one evening. Not then had I ever eaten, nor have I yet, any mouthful of cake that was half as sweet and toothsome as was that she brought us. Corn bread is good but it does not adequately nourish growing tissue. We always had enough food of the kinds we could get, but we were never fully nourished. Sugars and fats and proteins were lacking. I recall our hunger for such foods and our envy of those who were better fed.

I must pay tribute here to two women of the Adventist faith.

My Aunt Marinda—Mother's sister—read an Adventist paper, *The Signs of the Times*. She had no other printed matter and she pored over, absorbed, and accepted as gospel truth every sentence of this. She thought that if it was in print, it must be true. She talked about it to us and others until all were weary and some impatient. One spring she knew that the world would soon come to an end. She summed it all up and proved it once too often; another sister, Aunt Amanda, sitting by the

33

fireplace, said, "Well, Rin, I do hope it don't happen till peaches get ripe; I'd like mighty well to have one more mess of cobbler." Aunt Marinda looked the disgust she could not speak.

One time I had such a bad stone bruise that I thought my whole foot would drop off. Aunt Marinda adopted me for her boy for the duration. She attended to that foot of mine with true skill and warm sympathy. It got well and I could run again.

Aunt Sally Smith lived a mile nearer town, really out of the Dry Fork area. She, too, was an Adventist. She had "read the Bible through on her knees," it was said. The Smiths were thrifty as they could be on that flat land. One vivid memory of this woman has lost no lustre through all the intervening years. On a day when Christmas was approaching, she walked the mile or more over frozen knobby ground, down lanes, over fences, and across fields to bring a basket of cookies and popcorn balls (by then we knew of popcorn) so that our mother could have something, however small, to brighten the birthday of Jesus, Friend of all the poor. We were hungry for sweets and for sympathy and she fed us; we were in prison on Dry Fork and she visited us.

Some pioneer must have built the one-room log house remembered as the Tom Finty cabin. In the woods not far away were the ruined remains of a charcoal pit. The house may have been twenty years old when we moved in and had not been occupied for a year. The floor had to be reinforced and made whole by the addition of several boards from the loft above, which left half of a clapboard roof and the rafters of rough saplings visible from below. There were two doors, one at the east and one at the west; the west one had no hinges and the other would not shut tight. The one window had only a single sash and could not be opened, but there was plenty of ventilation.

It was a poor enough place to live, but our memory of that period of homelessness and the ambling covered wagon made

34

any sort of shelter good enough. The Smiths and Irvines and Uncle Jimmy Sons had much better houses, to be sure, but that troubled us not at all; that is, it did not trouble us young ones. I heard a lament from my mother's lips once when we lived there that has pathetic meaning and causes a heart pang as I recall it now. She had been helping Mrs. Smith—Aunt Sally, we called her—at house cleaning. She walked the mile morning and evening and brought home her scant pay in some form of food for the table. One evening at supper, after such a day, she sighed and said, wearily, as much to herself as to us, "When I go away where folks have things nice and comfortable and come back home this way, I get so discouraged I don't know what to do." The deep pathos of that lament hurts me still.

Our furniture at that time consisted of a table, two bedsteads, four or five chairs, including the wide rocker, two stoves, and a kerosene lamp with no flue. For three full years we had no lamp flue or money to buy one—there were things we needed so much more. When darkness came, we could go to bed.

Our cookstove was a real antique. But it served its own good purpose and another as well. On the cast iron hearth of it were the words "Bridge Brothers and Beach, St. Louis, Mo." My sister and I taught the twins their first lessons in the alphabet from that stove hearth when they were four years old. The letters O B R and S occurred three times; I A and T twice, D G H N C L U M once, while a larger list, F J K P Q V W X Y and Z, were not in the curriculum at all.

Our books were an ancient, musty-smelling Bible, originally bound in black leather but with one of its covers missing; and a book about the great plains, called *The Buffalo Land*. Later we secured two more books from somewhere, a *History of Andersonville Prison* and *Robinson Crusoe*. We borrowed the county newspaper when we could and read it, usually three weeks late.

35

A few issues of the *Youth's Companion* came to us from some source and we read every word in them. John Thomas insisted on lending us the *Book of Mormon* and in summer, when days were long and dull, my mother would lie on a quilt under one of the beds, to keep away from the too-friendly house flies, while I read to her through respect for John Thomas who was a kind-hearted neighbor. My mother pronounced that book a hoax and I was glad, for I did not like to read it.

The "big storm" came when I was ten. We had recently moved into the Tom Finty cabin. The west door that lacked hinges we kept propped up with a board. When the storm broke one evening after dark, down went that door and out went our oil lamp. Then the one sash of our one window crashed. For what seemed a long hour the tornado swept through our home without cessation. Great trees came crashing down in the woodland about us. Broken branches filled the air. The flash of lightning was continuous and clap after clap of thunder made the night a terror to us all. We took refuge under the beds. In the midst of it, in a momentary pause, I heard my mother's voice in prayer. "Oh, God, be merciful and save us all," she said fervently. It was the first time I had heard her pray. Kind neighbors came in the morning to learn how it had fared with the "widder." We had been exposed to merciless forces and frightened beyond measure; we had slept in damp beds; our house, poor at best, was hardly fit to live in. But the sun came out clear and warm over it all and quiet reigned. And I, because I had heard my mother's prayer, believed God had saved us. I believe so still.

The next year we moved up in the world—to a hewed-log house a mile away, where there was a lean-to kitchen, a half-story room upstairs, and a well. Until then we had never had drinking water nearer than a mile except in winter when wet-weather springs were flowing. Our house was farther down the creek, near where Whiteoak flowed into Wash Branch.

I, the fisher boy of the family, welcomed the move for there were deeper pools and, presumably at least, bigger fish in Wash Branch. Here we had a fireplace. We had had one before, but it had a chimney built of sticks and clay and might catch fire at any time; in fact, it did once. We had, moreover, two windows of two sashes each and an upstairs with a low roof where a bed might be set up under the clapboard roof. Across one creek lived David Mills; across the other Jackson Windland and Aunt Nancy; not far away John Thomas and Uncle David Truax. These were kindly people, humble and poor, but not poor like us, for they owned land and had houses of their own to live in.

While we were living in the Tom Finty house, David Mills decided to build a new house. Since we had two rooms with a loft and only six in the family, he asked for the privilege of living with us, with his four, during late winter and early spring. My memory of that period is very vivid for one sole reason. Our seasonal guests brought with them a flock of geese. Boys in our community always hid out all the eggs they could lay hands on the week before Easter and brought them in for Easter morning breakfast. That is all we then knew about Easter. We had but a dozen hens, so I found few eggs, but I had discovered a goose nest below the garden. Before incubation began, I braved the fearsome hissings of the ugly old goose and stole one of the eggs. I decided that I would not bring it in with the others but would cook it for myself later in the day; so down on the creek bank in a secluded place I built a fire and boiled that egg in a tin can. As it cooked, I threw in a hook and caught a sunfish, for the day was fresh and warm. When the egg was done and the fish broiled on a pointed stick, I salted them to taste and proceeded with my solitary repast. I got by with the sunfish and began on the egg. There I met inglorious defeat. When I had done my best, even to mild nausea, I flung two thirds of that egg into

37

the creek and went ruefully back to the house. If I would do justice to that exploit, I must borrow a figure from William Dean Howells, "From that day to this my symbol for inexhaustible abundance is a boiled goose egg." Only his was fried.

Uncle Billy Beck used to come over on foot occasionally in winter. He would bring us a roll of periodicals, one called *The Christian,* which afterward became and still is *The Christian-Evangelist.* He would sit by our patched-up cast-iron stove a while, chat with my mother, pat the twins on the head, and then take leave. Sometimes, then, he would come back, knock on the door, as though by afterthought, and say, "Jane, I almost forgot this sack of potatoes I set down here at the door; we have more than we need. Mary thought you might be able to use them." It was he who dropped his arm about my shoulders when, four years later, I confessed faith in Christ as the Son of God, and said to me, "Sammy, you have done a noble thing tonight."

Uncle Billy's papers were not to be returned. When we had read them, Mother would make paste of flour (unless we were in a corn-meal or shorts depression) and cover the rough walls of our cabin as best she could with them. With her dim eyes she could not be sure the print was right side up. Consequently, often when a hungry-minded lad, sleeping late, or kept in bed by ague chills, started to read something he had missed or wished to read a second time, he would have to loosen the paper to get the conclusion from the other side or maybe stand on his head to finish.

Two hungers of my life went unsatisfied in the log-house period. One was the desire for a good pocketknife, the other for books and reading matter. And my two extravagances in later life have been prompted by this still-insatiable desire. I have a half dozen knives lying around in addition to the pet one I carry with me—the one brought to me from Vienna, Austria, by a grandson. And I have books everywhere, in the cases near me as I write, in a room at Leatherwood Farm, up-stairs, and in the basement, on tables in every room, and stuck away in every conceivable place. I sometimes decide to get rid of a lot of things. But when I look over my knives to choose one for some boy, I can't decide which of them I prize least; or if I decide to enrich the library of some preacher, I find my-self reluctant to let go a single one of my long-time book friends.

One neighbor had a son, a year younger than I, with whom I played occasionally. One Sunday in that home I spied a bit of a bookshelf built in between a door and a window and my interest rose to fever heat. At the earliest possible moment, when I was alone in the room, I made invoice of the contents. The few volumes were all school textbooks except two; one was some sort of government report in fine print and uninteresting to a boy, the other was a book on natural history. I asked my playmate to show me that book and he did so hesitantly; it was full of pictures of fishes and animals and birds in color. I was thrilled. I resolved to borrow that book; everybody lent books if they had them, as few did, indeed, and nobody besides my mother's family ever returned a book. But as I buried my nose in that one, much to the surprise of my playmate who wanted to go fishing, the father came into the room and said gruffly, in a tone that angers me still, "You boys put up that book and let things alone that are none of your business." That was his attitude toward boys and books then and always. He kept his book nice and clean.

Periodically my mother would start us on reading the Bible. We would be gathered about our table, the little flueless oil lamp our only light. We took turns reading. The words were often hard; the print was small, and our light poor. We did not understand much that we read, nor did our mother, I sup-pose, but because she thought the Bible ought to be read, and because we had no other evening occupation, we read it. My mother preferred the Psalms. She seemed to get more from poetry of praise than from solemn and interminable prose with its hard names and extended genealogies.

Our mother could explain some things to us. When I came upon the letters A.D. and asked her, she said they stood for *anno domini;* and when I asked her what that meant, she said it meant "the year of our Lord." I did not know what "the year of our Lord" meant, for I did not then know who our Lord was. We had a saying, applied to coffee sometimes, "as strong as ackafortis." She told us it meant "strong water." I remembered that, as I seem to have remembered everything that related to language or literature. But it was a long time before I found the right words, *aqua fortis.* It was a long and difficult way, out of the dense ignorance and universal sordidness of Dry Fork and into the marginal lands of even ordinary intelligence.

One young fellow told me all about the Bible as we were hulling hazelnuts. He was An Williamson, a lewd, dirty fellow some years my senior, who knew nothing and thought he knew everything. He said, "Sam, I bet you don't know where the Bible came from." I admitted that I did not. "Well," said he, with the flourish of many an ignoramus I have met since, "I'm a goin' to tell you, an' I don't want you ever to fergit it." He assumed a cocksure attitude and went on; he said, "God wrote it all down on a big rock with his forefinger." I have heard a good many men settle that question in ways as satisfactory to them as was An Williamson's to him.

An Williamson! I have met him often, sometimes in a fundamentalist group, sometimes posing as a modernist. But wherever I find him, he is always as dogmatic as he was that day. I hear him with respect as a rule, but always reach for the salt shaker.

I met with another difficulty in biblical exegesis—a problem

40

of textual criticism it proved to be—and which was finally settled to my complete satisfaction.

I had read the story of Zacchaeus and the tree with very great interest. I had even laughed a little, though reading the Bible; it was always funny to me to watch a short-legged man in a hurry to get someplace. But there was no difficulty in that; it was his tree-climbing that stumped me. All the sycamores I had ever seen had big, smooth trunks and were very tall—twenty feet to the first limb. I could climb any tree anyone else could, at least I thought I could. But how a rich man, like Zacchaeus, who undoubtedly would wear shoes, could climb a tree like that with his short legs was beyond me. I disliked to doubt anything in the Bible; my mother thought that was wrong, so I did not tell her of my doubts. Nearly twenty years later a preacher friend of mine, extolling the merits of Luther's version of the New Testament, called my attention to the rendering there; it is not sycamore but mulberry! I had climbed mulberry trees in the woods and had seen the low, domestic kind. Anybody could climb that kind of tree!

I have no sentiment at all about log houses. I have one on a little plot of ground where the babbling waters of Leatherwood Creek flow. To make it livable in a later age it has had to be weatherboarded, lined inside, papered, and underpinned. The log houses served when nothing better was to be had. They were typical of an era. We associate them and the open fireplace with robust living, good morals, and a wholesome social life in a time of simple enjoyments. As places of human habitation they were but refuges from sun and storm until something better might be had. The fireplace was a good social artifice but useful for warming purposes only when supplemented by steam heat or its equivalent.

The trouble with the log houses of Dry Fork was that their

people went in no direction. They were dug in and did not know the directions. Thus, standing still, they became stagnant with unexpressed goodness which so easily becomes badness, or fermented and ran over with uncurbed vicious impulse in the way men call criminal.

One distinct and important purpose the log houses rendered. They turned out a persistent and enduring type of human being. Many who knew such humble experience in early life rise to other levels presently. These help others and themselves survive when the reverses of life befall. They know how to bear up and be hopeful in the face of hardship and misfortune. They have seen worse days.

Chapter 4

Economic Pressure on Dry Fork

My first job thrills me yet. I ran home to tell my mother about it; Mr. Hill would give me a half bushel of sweet potatoes if I would come and pick them up for him as he forked them from the ground. "You run right back and tell him you'll do it," she said, "you'll soon be one of my main helpers." I was seven then. I surmised that the man had improvised the task for me; but he did have lumbago and it hurt him to stoop. That did not matter; my mother praised me. I was beginning to help the family.

Then came the hard days. My sister and I might be able to secure from five to seven days' work each summer dropping corn. Once in a while we got in a day of weeding or carrying water to harvest hands for which we received twenty-five cents a day. Our elder brother did better; he might get fifty cents in harvest and threshing time.

Our mother supplemented the scant income with what she could earn by house cleaning or washing clothes for neighbors within walking distance. She had to work twice as hard as would anyone who had good eyesight to make sure the result of her toil would bear inspection. Through many a long summer day, two of us kept the twins in Mother's absence and looked forward to evening when she came home, usually carrying a bag of breadstuff or other eatables as her wage.

There was no pension for the blind, no widow's pension, no orphan allowances, no social security, and no arrangement for relief in those days. We earned what we ate and ate only what we earned, though it was the cheapest and plainest of food—corn bread or shorts bread, which was not as good, and potatoes, with fruit in season when there was fruit and a bite or two of meat now and then.

My sister worked in homes for a brief season occasionally, where there was illness or a new baby. She received the standard pay for a girl who did a woman's work—fifty cents a week. There would seem to have been very little money in circulation then. Often we had to wait weeks for our wages and maybe go and ask for it then. We were far out on the extreme of the financial system.

The region produced enough food to feed its people, but it was not evenly distributed. Some who worked half as hard as we had twice as much to eat. But it never occurred to us to whimper or complain. We were low in the social scale, to be sure, and through no fault of our own. But we were too busy making a living and trying to get forward a little to waste time lamenting.

Our mother, once a Quaker girl in Morgan County, Ohio, had had to quit school at fifteen. Her eyesight, as already mentioned, had begun to bother her then. There was nothing to be done about it but to accept the inevitable, after home remedies had failed and the calomel-quinine family physician had pronounced his worthless verdict. She could not have known what her loss would mean in after years and the progress of the infirmity was so slow and gradual that she adapted herself to life conditions without difficulty or complaint. Once or twice, only, did I hear her express regret but I knew all along that

44

she nursed an unuttered but rankling resentment that she had not been able to secure even such education as was available in her youth. She insisted always, and with inflexible determination, that no child of hers should miss a day's schooling if she could help it. And many a hard sacrifice did she make for us during those dark, dragging days.

It was my privilege, when her eyesight was gone, to spend a day with her in the clinic of the ablest oculist in the Mississippi Valley, while thorough examination was being made. Done with it, the good man took both her hands in his and said, "I wish I could give you a better report, Mother—you have one of the finest pairs of eyes I have ever seen; but you can never see; it is the optic nerve that has suffered injury."

Then instantly she asked, "Could it ever have been cured?"

His answer, "No, we have little knowledge of it and no remedy even now."

Again, and with a tremor in her voice, "Is it likely to occur again in the family?"

He knew what she meant and with a quick side glance at me, said, "No, my good woman, there need be no fear of that."

She was relieved and ever afterward was a happier woman.

That was a memorable day to me. From earliest years I had dreamed of a time when I could know certainly the facts about that mysterious affliction my mother had borne so patiently. After the meticulous examination was over, we went together through the business streets and variety stores of Cincinnati. I tried to describe to her the merchandise on display. Many things she took in her hands and by that attenuated sense of touch she "saw" them as well as, for years at least, she could see anything. Then, waiting at the station, she spoke words of tender appreciation to me, "I am glad for this day. I know now I can never see, but I know this affliction will not be visited on my children or on any who come after; and I am satisfied."

When the eldest of us, then aged seventeen, had to go north to husk corn so that we might have bread, it was a matter of deepest concern to our mother—deeper, I am certain, than she ever allowed us to suppose. She knew he would get no more schooling; her heart's sympathy followed the lone son so early thrust out to take a man's place in the world.

I recall that dire day when he packed such clothes as he would take with him in the old black valise we had always kept under a bed. Mother was unusually quiet as we ate breakfast. There was no emotion on her part when he left and went whistling up the road toward town, but she stood by the door and tried shading her dim eyes with a hand to see him as long as she could. I noticed that the whistling stopped when he turned into the woods, and I wondered why. When the day came for me to go up that road, or one much like it, I discovered how hard it is to whistle when one turns into the woods.

We had planted a patch of late potatoes in a clearing that summer. They had no attention and we had forgotten them. One rainy evening my sister and I, passing that way from school, kicked a fine big tuber out of the soft ground. We went running home to tell Mother. The next Saturday we dug them, six bushels of as fine potatoes as could be desired. We buried that treasure in the garden, an economic backlog of generous dimensions.

Every two weeks we walked to town, my sister and I, to get from the mails the small remittance we knew would come from our absent breadwinner. We would buy the indispensables— sugar, rice, and coffee—and trudge home again arriving usually at dark. We got through that winter somehow but it was a critical period as every winter on Dry Fork was.

Once our rich relatives at Xenia, twenty miles away, sent us a Christmas box. It contained unsalable but useful goods from the store, partly worn garments and some staple groceries. I still remember my embarrassment when I was sent to Oak

46

Valley Sunday School wearing, out of that box, a pair of women's shoes, too large for me, with high heels, and laced at the side.

Again our mother so conquered her sensitiveness as to take us all to Xenia in a farm wagon, a borrowed horse paired with Old Charley. It was but fair and just, I think our mother reasoned, that two prosperous merchants should know how it fared with the orphaned brood of their younger brother. The two uncles rose to the occasion with commendable generosity. We were fitted out with winter boots and shoes from regular stock and not made to feel that we were beggars. They were good men after the fashion of the time and place.

It was then I came into possession of my first pair of brass-toed boots. On the way home I dropped off behind the wagon several times to walk in the dust and admire the clear-cut tracks I made. I contrasted them, as I walked proudly along, with those of my bare feet that had never quite satisfied me. It seemed to me to be another long step toward respectability.

On that visit to Xenia occurred a keenly embarrassing incident. The twins were unable as yet to talk intelligibly to all, but I could understand them. After supper on the first evening we were there, they began asking, in unison and most insistently, for a drink of water. I could interpret their babyish demand correctly, and did. But when water was brought in a tin cup, they both refused to drink. Between their wailings I discovered the reason, and when I did I faded away. They found me behind a lilac bush in the yard and walked me in to act as interpreter and quell the disturbance. The twins wanted to drink out of a glass tumbler, the like of which they had never seen until at that meal. I felt that family secrets were being ingloriously revealed, and it hurt me to have to unveil our humiliation.

There was very little money in circulation on Dry Fork. At twelve I had had exactly fifteen cents to spend for myself and as I

47

pleased to spend it. I bought a pair of suspenders with a dime of my capital and with the nickel a lead pencil with an eraser on it. The suspenders were gay in color and smelled of elastic webbing; another step upward, I reasoned. The pencil was just a pet. I had no use for it. We had no blank paper save that used for wrapping purchases brought from town and that was so dark that my pencil had no chance of distinction through performance on its surface. I did find two or three blank pages in *Buffalo Land* and covered them with my compositions, erasing and then writing again until there were holes here and there in my manuscript.

One summer when corn was knee high, a nearby farmer offered my sister and me a dollar to cut the sprouts out of a two-acre plot of new ground. He was, we had been led to believe, a benevolent type of man. The fall before he had given us several shocks of corn fodder for Old Cherry. We understood that he was a church member, occasionally attending the Sunday afternoon services at Dry Fork schoolhouse. That was before dollars had been deflated. The one we were to have would be of silver and as big as a dinner plate. Certainly it would buy a great deal; we had never had that much money. How we two worked at that job! Our tools were the most primitive—the old dull ax and the hoe that would not stay on the handle. But, though it took days of wearisome chopping and slashing, we were done at last. Sweaty and dust-begrimed, we trudged past the farmer's house, a quarter of a mile out of the way, as we went home. We thought he might pay us. We lingered at his well, a luxury we did not then possess, drinking more water than even our thirsty bodies required, in the hope that we might attract his attention. Finally, one of us ventured to the kitchen door and announced that we were done. Nothing came of that and we trudged down the hill and across the Whiteoak toward home. In the days that followed we indulged much impatient wishing, but no dollar came. Then, at Mother's insistence, we went to ask for the money. And the farmer made answer, "Why, I considered that had been paid long ago."

When we told Mother, she donned her sunbonnet and, in a mood we had never before observed, took her way resolutely across the creek and up the hill. Not knowing what else to do, I followed. Much else that happened on Dry Fork comes back but dimly to me, but that interview is a livid and frightful memory to this day. My mother asked the man bluntly and with an ominous overtone when that dollar had been paid. He gave her a quick look and backed toward the well curb. Then he said, "Why, Mrs. Lappin, it was paid with that fodder I let you have for your cow last fall." It was there my mother took over. The blitzkrieg was no new thing when the dictators made use of it. My mother understood the technique fifty years ago. But it was unavailing, for the dollar was never paid. The families were not on speaking terms after that. Those who hitherto had been playmates when returning from school together walked on opposite sides of the road. I know how feuds start; and I am no stranger to the dark passions that promote and perpetuate them. Nearly every year I drive past the now worn-out farm where we did that bit of hard labor without reward; often I meet the second or third generation of that man's descendants, but I always think of the unpaid dollar and silently pray to be kept humble, unvengeful, forgiving.

The "bad year" and the "big wheat year" came during our six years' sojourn on Dry Fork. In that part of Illinois there had to be a copious shower once a week on the average if crops were to thrive. It is not the fault of soil or subsoil, but lying out of sight between the two is a layer of impervious clay called "hardpan." In winter the accumulated wetness above becomes mud. In summer the moisture soon evaporates. Dust and dryness result and plant life wilts and withers. There was always fear of drouth in cropping season.

49

One summer was unlike all others in this respect. There was no rain at all from corn-planting time until near autumn. That was "locust year" too. The swarm that had gone down seventeen years before came up, every single individual of them, it would seem, as answering a summons, and came up "singing." As the drouth became more and more serious and corn, not yet knee-high, withered in the fields, chinch bugs appeared and finished the crop completely. Then locusts in all the woodland tracts sent up the loudest and most strident whirring chorus ever heard by any living resident in the locality. Creeks slowed down, stopped running, and then went entirely dry. Mud turtles were found even in dusty roads, leaving the waterless deep holes and legging it off toward the next nearest and deepest as though guided by a radio beam. Wells went lower and lower until not one in a dozen had water to spare for stock, many not for family use. Forest trees shed their leaves in late July and August. Public funds for relief were exhausted. Visitors from Ohio begged their relatives to give it up and go back with them to a better country. Of eatable growths only persimmons and pumpkins were plentiful, and all of us learned how little nutriment they contain and how unpalatable they can become.

However, human life does not accept defeat with ready grace. When it was so late in the season that it seemed ridiculous, rains came and gardens were replanted. Then a vast acreage of wheat was put in. The late plantings produced bountifully. Frost held off until potatoes could be dug. There was food in abundance, such as it was. Peach trees bloomed in September and when first frosts came in October, the fruit was half grown. Mother Nature seemed to be in an apologetic mood toward her children.

Bounteous relief came next year. The soil had stored up the power of the sun from a previous season and poured it out in rich reward to the children of men; and there was seasonal rain. Everywhere waved rich golden grain—it was the "big wheat year"—with tall, well-filled heads of plump and fat grains. Unusual rains fell until the grain was fully ripe. Then to get it all harvested was the problem. There was a shortage of field hands and no one was idle that year. We had five acres. Because of stumps, it had to be cut with cradle, raked and bound by hand, and put in shock for threshing. While my older brother was working for wages elsewhere, an uncle came on a Sunday to swing the cradle and we put it in shock that day, the only Sunday but one that I ever worked at manual labor.

In preparation for that day's work there had to be food for our harvesters. But the family exchequer showed no balance. There was no surplus among neighbors that could be borrowed. That was our mother's problem, and she met it. Mounting Old Charley, she rode to Geff, five miles away. I doubt if she could have gone there, left to herself, but the horse knew the exact place to stop at a hitchrack in front of Bestow's store when he was headed in that direction, and from that location Mother could find the door. She knew Uncle Johnny Bestow. He, too, was a Buckeye. She laid her case before him and he let her have needed supplies to the value of less than five dollars, with no other assurance than her word that it would ever be paid. That got us through the harvest.

I do not know what became of our wheat. But it is a vivid enough memory that we, who had eaten corn bread for the six months past, were suddenly reveling in pancakes, biscuits, and lightbread such as only our mother could make.

For reasons that must have been sufficient the bill at Bestow's store was not paid. More than once in my childhood I heard my mother voice a bitter regret over this. She had made special appeal to a mere acquaintance for accommodation in an emergency and it had been granted. She had failed to make good. There had never been money for it, but that did not heal the smarting of a sensitive conscience. The groceryman sent no reminder and the rest of us forgot it, but my mother never did.

One day, long after Uncle Johnny Bestow had died, when the small estate he left had been used up, when his only living son, a man well past middle life, began to find subsistence at home a daily problem, my mother with a little money at her disposal at last paid that bill, explaining it all in the letter she sent with her post office money order. She was totally blind then and eighty years old, living comfortably with her daughter, and pensioned by her sons. She had no response to her letter but she had the answer of a good conscience.

My mother did that, as I know, because she was a Christian. Early in young womanhood she had committed herself to that way of life. All through the grief and bitterness of her widowhood she had held steadfastly to the vows of her youth and to what they implied.

Chapter 5

The Educational Process on Dry Fork

The two older children had had some schooling in the Ozarks. Pleasant Hope in Polk County had a better school by far than that we attended intermittently at Hardscrabble on Dry Fork. But I had been too young, too small, too puny to walk the two and a half miles over stony hillside roads. I had to get my schooling at home, looking at pictures in the outgrown books of the older ones and spelling words for my mother to pronounce.

It was a surprise to the family when I announced that I had read McGuffey's *Third Reader* through three times and had begun on the fourth. I must have been five years old then. In the three years that followed I read every second, third, and fourth reader I could get hold of, but had not spent a day in school nor had an hour of instruction from anyone but my mother, herself blind and unschooled.

The day came, however, in the spring of the second summer on Dry Fork when my mother said to me on a Friday, "Sam, you'll have to go to school on Monday." That was a veritable black Friday to me and a "lost week end." I did not want to go to school; I never have. But there was no appeal from that decision. I was afraid—afraid to go and afraid not to go.

A pair of slow-moving, reluctant feet trod the woodland path that morning. They were tough, brown, bare feet, well used to running, jumping, and climbing, but that day the will to move was paralyzed by fear. Mating birds were alert and calling among the trees; Johnny-jump-ups and spring beauties were pushing their lovely heads through the leaf mold; I could hear the joyous caroling of frogs down by the branch in my customary playground. I had to leave all this, and go to school. I was a pathetic child pioneer, leaving his preliminary of play and pushing out into a world of duty and obligation.

Timidity and bashfulness made me afraid that day. I was not afraid of the teacher, a neighbor's daughter; nor of the pupils, for I had seen several of them at one time or another; nor of the books, for I loved books and always have. I was just afraid of the new world I was entering with no knowledge of what lay ahead. *I did not want to go to school,* for I was afraid; but I was more afraid of what might be waiting at home if I turned back. So I went on.

On the long two and a half miles to school my spirits went down, down, down as I took each step. When I arrived, I hid from the other children at play, lingering out of sight in the hazel brush until the teacher's bell called the urchins in. Then I crept shyly out of hiding and across the playground to the schoolhouse door. As I peeped fearfully round the casing, the teacher saw me and came to put her perfumed arm about me tenderly and lead me to a seat. "We have a new pupil this term," she said, and told my name. Then she gave me a book and I was at home and happy. Most of my fears have vanished thus quickly; but I am still afraid of things new to me.

We had two major amusements on the playground; they were "drop the handkerchief" and "black man." I thought the teacher paid special attention to me; she nearly always dropped the handkerchief behind me. And I imagined she loved me more than any other. I know now, and humbly confess it here, that it was because she knew *I needed to be loved* more than the rest.

I resolved to marry that teacher when I should be old enough. I did marry her husband's youngest sister, as happened; and that is a good deal nearer than I usually come to fulfilling my resolutions.

We took our dinners to school since it was too far to go home for food. Some brought neat baskets with clean napkins. Some brought a piece of bread and meat wrapped in paper. Two families of big boys provided great buckwheat pancakes, skillet-size, well-buttered, rolled up tightly and carried, end of the roll down, in an outside coat pocket. I can see that ruffian bunch yet, each one hungrily biting at one end of his great brown roll of buckwheat and butter. In nothing else was the differing economic status of Dry Fork homes so clearly marked as in the lunches brought to Hardscrabble school.

There were many fights on the playground—slight differences were quickly settled and some, those thought to be more serious, were decided on a level spot of ground up the creek farther from the schoolhouse. There was education, even in that. Dan Shell and Jim Golliher were our champions during the summer term I attended there. They never clashed with one another. That, in the minds of those younger, would have been a major engagement—a battle of giants. To them was allotted the job of settling the differences between smaller boys and preserving an enduring peace. When a fracas seemed imminent, the principals were taken to that small arena up the creek and allowed to fight it out, each with his champions looking on. The system worked well. Fistic performance did not last long when properly publicized and the principals usually came back friends.

Toward the end of a summer term, dark and ominous clouds began to threaten. It was rumored that trouble had risen between the champions, that Dan Shell and Jim Golliher, our two heroes, were to go up the creek on the last day of school. We younger ones spoke of that prospect with bated breath. Certainly that would be a struggle of titanic dimensions for we all believed that nobody on earth could lick either of these tough fellows. The day came and dragged along with deep mutterings until the last recess. Then, when the teacher's disciplinary measures would be out of the question, came the lull before the battle. Up the creek went Jim, walking with swagger and bravado, his admirers following, pale around the gills. Came, then, Dan, his bevy of awed urchins about him.

There, on the scene of many a boyish tussle stood Jim Golliher, trembling (with rage, as we supposed) and rolling up his sleeves as for combat and carnage. But the coming of Dan was too much for him. He just could not stand it. He turned and ran, fleet as a frightened fawn. Unwilling to pursue, for, as I have no doubt, he too was badly scared, Dan let loose a small stone he had been carrying. It clipped a leaf or two as it sailed into a graceful upward curve and, descending, struck Jim on the temple, felling him like a shot. Dan, terrified at what he had done, ran to where Jim lay and said in a deep, throaty voice, as he bent over him, "Jim, I didn't go to do it; honest I didn't, Jim." And then, turning to the rest he said fiercely, "Don't any of you dare tell the teacher." And we did not dare. Jim and Dan came back to the schoolyard friends.

Certain accompaniments of the learning process at Hardscrabble in winter were such as are seldom mentioned in good literature. But this book is more a confession than a mere record, so it must face facts squarely, though they be unsavory. Sooner or later every pupil got lice, itch, and sore eyes. Of course, I had them all but never more than one at a time. Taking them singly, rather than in unison, gave variety to the whole winter term of four months. If measles or mumps or chicken pox came, that made one-a-month for the entire time; but these contagious things were impediments and kept us out of school, as the others did not. Our mother was a competent home doctor. Besides soda in water, which I think she might have prescribed for a sore toe, her three main remedies then were salt, sulphur, and red precipitate. These singly and in combination—hot lard being added in certain cases—did the business. For itch it was sulphur and lard; for lice, red precipitate and lard. In the case of head lice, the noxious ointment had to be backed up with a fine-toothed comb rigorously applied to the tender scalp, the lesser ones of her brood on knees before her. But it came to be noted that Widder Lappin's children were always rid of these community contaminations ahead of any others in Hardscrabble school.

Friendship quilts were in style then. The great-aunt who gave us our cow pieced a block of white and indigo blue muslins for me. I proudly carried it to school and started it round among the girls. One by one my collection grew. But, dire tragedy to the heart of a boy, the style changed and my quilt did not take shape until forty years later when, while teaching in Bethany College, my remarkable mother-in-law took the matter in hand and assembled the scant number of parts I had kept into an old model. I have it yet, a few squares pieced out of ancient calicos and ginghams, abundantly "set together" with unduly large squares of more modern fabric and assembled by hands that had fully finished the unnumbered tasks of a long and busy life. When I look at that quilt, it speaks to me of good will and of that finer, higher quality we call love.

Pet Cariens, my childhood sweetheart, was the best speller in my class. I was the poorest. How I did wish I might get one head mark—just one, if only to keep in good standing with her! But never could I get one. I would hold my place day by day while others achieved and "went foot" and then when, if only I could get by another recitation, I would have a head mark, some other pupil, usually Pet Cariens, would spell a word I had missed and "go" head.

Nobody ever taught me how to learn to spell. I would rattle over the words a hundred times, never noticing the relation of the letters or how the word looked as a whole. I did not learn to spell until I began writing for publication and noticed the appearance of words. In common with most I have learned, I mastered it when need came.

There were four months of school in winter and two in summer. After the one summer term at Hardscrabble, we moved into Ward School District; but the process was the same there, and everywhere, so far as I know. Our textbooks were not uniform; we took what we had and the teacher somehow managed to get along. That pleased me, for I got to read a half dozen different readers where, had the books been uniform, I should have had but one. And we learned to compare Barnes's history with Montgomery's, Harvey's grammar with Holbrook's, Ray's arithmetic with White's, and so on down the list. With what help the teacher could give, pupils gathered from this array of books the learning available in rural areas at that time. There were no tests or written examinations, and no such process as grading. At the close of a term an "exhibition" would be given so that pupils could show off a little before their parents.

The system had some excellent advantages. Pupils had to dig for what they got. They learned to ask for help only in the last extremity. Books and reading matter were so scarce that there was a normal hunger for them. The long walk to and from school and the hours spent doing chores afforded ample time for reflection and calling again to memory what had been once in the mind. Our reading books were idealistic. They held up good models. They inspired the pupil to look higher. The things studied and learned had definite purpose. Near at hand could be found place to apply it all. The McGuffey series of readers and their near kin, the blue-backed speller, and Ray's *Third Part*, all things considered, have never been excelled.

58

I presume some things are the same today. I understand the multiplication table has not been thrown into discard. But much else, that is fully as vital to human life and peace on earth among men of good will, has been lost, or what is the same, buried in the plethora of pedagogical theory and wholly useless pseudo-psychological guesswork.

One teacher in Ward School told us in a moment of pause that he had been on a train that "traveled sixty miles an hour." We sat open-mouthed and incredulous at that.

Many unconventional activities are educational. Whoever does anything well—and especially if he has to teach himself to do it—is acquiring education. The bane of most schoolwork has been that it was so arranged and so offered to the learner that it was odious to begin with. We progress by learning to do difficult things. But the difficulty of it is nil if they are things we enjoy doing or if we do them under the stimulus of a challenge.

There was something to be learned as a boy roamed the woods for nuts or mulberries; as he sounded the pools of Wash Branch for catfish or waded for mussels; as he built and set traps for quail and rabbits in winter time.

Or it might be in early spring when a boy's first enjoyment is the making of whips and whistles. One had to discover when the sap came up, what kind of hickory withe to choose for a whip; what size and length of wood for the kind of whistle he wanted. It took a sharp knife, and careful use of it, to trim and prepare the stick, and skill of hand to make the whistle or plait the whip.

At a little later date for fishing I had to find bait, to prepare lines, sinkers, and corks, to select a suitable pool, to know where sunfish might be found and where catfish lurked on the bottom, to be skilled in the handling of pole and line, guessing by the bite what sort of fish I might be about to land.

There was a time for bow and arrow. Then I sought from the woods a suitable piece of hickory for bow; from the crimson mulberry root tough bark for bowstring; from fields a stiff hard weed stem for arrow; from a tin can a triangular bit of tin to be bent and sharpened for a spud.

Then, autumn was the time for traps. I had no materials for a box trap. No one taught me to set a snare and I did not try to learn that, for it left the little creatures to suffer until I came to relieve their pain by death. My traps were built, wigwam shape, with slats of wood, a hickory bow tied down over the top to complete each unit. Then the figure-four triggers and bait of an apple core or a nubbin of corn for rabbits, or scattered wheat for quail. I usually had a half dozen traps set. My catch was never large, but with eager expectancy I made the rounds.

Exploring the wooded tracts along Wash Branch and Dry Fork, I somehow learned to know all the trees and shrubs. What meant more, I learned to love them and even now I find special relish in discovering a new species of wood growth of any kind. When my grown sons and grandsons ask me the name of a common tree, I realize what they have missed by not having a rural background.

Birds and their nests were of particular interest. I knew the names of birds, their nesting habits, and the color of their eggs. I have always respected the jay since one brought blood from my hand as I felt above me in a nest to learn what its egg was like. The doughty fellow chased me down the tree and cursed me in bird language until I was out of hearing. The "swamp robin," or chewink, or, as we named him, the "jo whang," intrigued me. A shy, suspicious dweller in remote woods, his call, like that of the wood thrush, has to me a witching quality, a languishing, sentimental note suggestive of solitude that takes me back far into the receding past.

Hornets I hated. More than once an enraged one, or, as I always thought, a crazy member of a colony, struck me near an eye like a pebble from a sling shot and left a sting that put that eye out of business for a time. Bumblebees I could endure, for they gave honey; but I could not see of what use hornets and wasps were or why they were created. I knew that bumblebees were useful only because my palate, starved for sweets, reveled in the nectar of their clustered cells. I fought out many a nest though I greatly feared the stings. I learned at the last, when other engagements were calling me, that a jug half-filled with water and set near the nest will lure and destroy every passing bee.

One Sunday I, with other lads, made war on a great colony of bumblebees in the hollow log of an old barn. The honey cells in that nest were unusually numerous and all well filled. We feasted on the contents, but something was wrong. It gagged us, hurt our throats, and sickened us. The bees had worked on the bloom of Jackson Windland's tobacco patch.

The pocketknife was my special joy, though I never had a good knife. I worked wonders with the old Barlow given me by a man who had worn its two blades to the halfway stage. I was an artificer. I could contrive and execute, even with my outworn old Barlow knife, things to wonder at. I spent hours that way and they were very happy hours. My masterpiece was a watch chain of thirteen links, a hook, a swivel and a charm, all from a bit of seasoned elm, and without the accident of a single split link. A watchmaker in the county seat saw that and examined it with his magnifying glass; then he looked at me and handed it back without a word, as though thinking, "I don't care what you say, there ain't any such animal."

All this, planned, designed, and wrought out in the long hours of leisure during our residence in the log houses on the headwaters of Dry Fork, was, as I now believe, a very important part of my education. It was manual training. I insist that it takes a quality of skill to put together two pieces of wood properly that is as fine and as essential as that required to combine colors in a picture or sentences in an essay, to solve mathematical problems, to play a musical instrument, or to operate a typewriter. And the actual inside gain in character and self-development may be as great in the one instance as in the other. That is why we have a great many well-educated folk who have had very little schooling and a large number of well-schooled ones who have very little education.

I was not able to cash in on any of the skills acquired on Dry Fork. I got no job on the strength of degrees there earned. But it was by that process, finally, that I got forward a little way in the world. What I know of Dry Fork and Wash Branch, even to this day, has been as worthwhile to me as what I know of Caesar's Gallic Wars or the Odes of Horace, read in translation long afterward. And it was the initiative and persistence learned in the accomplishment of my humble early projects that took me on into these other fields of delight.

All in all I had fourteen months of schooling during our residence on the tributaries of Dry Fork, not counting days missed on account of sickness and bad weather. But I had seven full years of education. That unquenchable thirst to know things, and more things, and still more things, has attended me to this day and is still a driving force in my life.

On the last day of my summer term at Hardscrabble I attempted to "recite my first piece." I knew the lines perfectly. It was from one edition of McGuffey's *Third Reader*. My recitation began with this couplet:

> The lark is up to meet the sun,
> The bee is on the wing. . . .

I got that far and things went black. My diaphragm bucked up inexplainably and my tongue clove to the roof of my mouth. I could not go on—could not utter another word. Choking and gasping I sat down in great confusion, the most astonished and surprised one in the whole crowd. I did not know what had happened to me. I could have said that bit of verse standing on my head. But there I was, dumb and in a blue funk. I am fairly familiar with that phenomenon now, though it has never happened to me in just that way since.

Out of that last day of school at Hardscrabble comes to me today as a strange, sweet fragrance, the memory of two songs that were sung. One was sung by a beautifully dressed girl of six or seven, daughter of a workman recently come from St. Louis. I had never seen clothes like those she wore; I had never known a child as pretty and vivacious. It was all like a dream to me—a vivid, beautiful dream, that first appearance of hers on the drab background of our school.

The other song was a sort of farewell that brought the program to a close. It stirred a tender, plaintive sentiment in me that has lived longer and kept sweeter in my heart than even the song of the little girl or any other song I have ever heard. I can recall but the languid refrain of it and the couplet. . . .

> The heart speaks most when the lips move not
> And the eye speaks a gentle good-bye.

That is true, everlastingly true. It is true to me this day and at this moment when, looking back through all the years, I speak my heart's good-bye to Dry Fork and Hardscrabble school and all that its experiences, both bitter and sweet, have meant to me on the long trail of life.

Chapter 6

There Came a Day

Something happens to a boy, or in a boy, at about the age of twelve. He begins to see the invisible. There came a day to me, on Dry Fork, unlike any other day that had ever been. The sun was brighter that day. Buds were unfolding with a fragrance rarer than ever scented earthly breeze. The call of birds in woodland and fence row was vibrant with unwonted witchery. Within myself stirred thoughts, resolves, intimations, convictions never experienced before. I did not understand it, nor do I now.

I would not always live on Dry Fork. Somehow I would get out of all that had occupied, entertained, depressed, and held me there. I did not know how it could be. I was too young to plan, just a stunted boy of twelve with all the vagrant and wayward tendencies and impulses of an irrepressible male child. Nobody had intimated any of this to me. There was no opening ahead, no prospect, no outlook, other than had been all along. But I would be getting out. I *knew* that. *How* I knew it or what would happen to bring it about I did not know.

I told it all to Old Charley, my head on his neck, as we jogged home from Jack Scott's where I had been sent on an errand. I whispered it to the spring beauties and Johnny-jump-ups on a green, mossy bank down by Wash Branch and bade them a tearful good-bye. I had no heart for fishing that day, though I had dug bait and brought out my fishing lines. There were other pools than these in waiting for me somewhere. These were shallow, slow-moving, muddy; those would be, when I found them, clear, deep, sparkling waters; and I would catch larger and better fish.

Word came to us that spring that a narrow-gauge railroad would be built across the country north of us. There would be work for men. Esquire Hawk and Major Stanley, known to us, were negotiating a grading contract. They might take on my elder brother. That would give him work but would leave us crippled for even the little farming we could do with our one horse. My mother did not like it and was very quiet for several days.

The thing took shape presently, and our brother drove away with the rest in a wagon carrying a load of plows, slip scrapers, hand tools, and a tent or two. Mother watched them go by, straining her dim eyes to see the vanishing form of her first-born. She shed no tears—I never knew her to shed a tear after the great grief that befell when her companion died.

What could we do about farming now? The time for planting corn was at hand. We even lagged and delayed with the garden beds usually laid out as snow melted and frosts became less frequent. Mother did not insist; her manner was strange to us. Day after day she seemed to be pondering deeply some decision she, of herself, must make.

One night she reached a conclusion and in the morning she made a startling announcement. We would sell out and join the railroad camp. That would be better than staying on Dry Fork as things were. There would certainly be something each one could do. It was a venture, but we would make it.

A man came to buy Old Charley. That is the one event that I remember best. Old Charley was one of the family. I took the prospective buyer to the log stable and led the horse out. The man eyed him critically and gave him a sharp kick in the side. Old Charley scampered in a semicircle, measured by the length of the halter rope, and then gave me a look of surprise while keeping an eye on the man who had come to buy him. He knew he was being sold; I am convinced of that. And I knew it with deep regret. The only reason I did not kick the man when he kicked our Old Charley was that I was not big enough. If he had done it again, I think I would have tried anyway.

We had to see Old Charley go and we saw through tears; he had been a constant friend to all of us. He was careful of the twins. If one fell from his back, he merely looked round and stood still until there was no danger of stepping on him. But it was not over when the gentle old fellow had gone to the drudgery of a new and unappreciative owner. On the Sunday that intervened we all walked to Oak Valley for a religious service—a sort of ceremonial farewell to Dry Fork. As we approached the little church in the woods where many horses were tied, we heard a loud, excited neigh; it was Old Charley. Two of us ran to him; he lowered his head for us with evident delight. We hugged him and again said a tearful farewell. Somewhere his bones may be bleaching today. Or perchance, in the economy of nature, they have been fed back into the soil. But if there are horses in heaven, which I would like to believe, no new breed would I ask, just a bay mustang pony with the letters "T H" on his right front shoulder and, for me, the task of supplying him with heavenly hay and celestial corn throughout all eternity.

We did not sell the cow. We might have to come back and in that case the cow would be needed. We let David Mills have her to pasture for the milk she would give and the calf she would presently bring.

The rest did not matter much. There was nothing else worth selling. Our humble household outfit went in a wagon driven by a neighbor going to join the camp. The five of us took our first train ride from Geff to Flora, the town nearest the camp, and caught a ride out to the vicinity of Sailor Springs where work was in progress. We were done with Dry Fork.

The ill-fated narrow gauge failed. Certain sections of the grade were well up to required level; others but half done; and over long spaces of the right-of-way, the soil was not broken. The work was held up by uncertainty. Anxious contractors and their men listened to rumors and waited. A few payments came dribbling in, followed by orders for goods at the stores in Flora; but at the summer's end everyone gave up and went home—the farmers to fields that had lain fallow and to cribs empty of corn.

We had escaped from Dry Fork only to become stranded on Indian Creek. My mother, with the aid of my sister, had kept boarders, supplying plain food to men made hungry by arduous muscular work in the open. The older brother, sharing the common misfortune, lost a large part of his summer's wages. Of course, the boarders could not pay, so the only course left was to stage a strategic retreat. This our mother decided to do.

As summer waned and prospects faded on Indian Creek, food became scarce at our house. My sister and I again had recourse to dropping corn by hand and covering it with hoes at twenty-five cents a day. Fruit and vegetables helped some. I got a few catfish from sloughs in the bottoms and my brother knew a spot in the Wabash where a fish trap was sunk at the end of a grapevine. But it was agreed that something had to be done before winter.

Then came a rumor. Mrs. Rapp, a merchantwoman in the little town of Geff, thirty miles away, and back toward Dry

Fork, needed a chore boy. The rumor told how she had asked an uncle of mine about his widowed sister and her family that used to live out on Dry Fork, mentioning a particular boy. I think it was that rumor that landed us at Geff. I was the boy in question. Many a time had I stolen furtively into that store to ask if I might have an almanac or an empty box. The proprietress had asked me questions about our family, showing a kindly interest; she, too, was a widow of about my mother's age, and when her son went to Lebanon, Ohio, to school, there was an opening for the chore boy.

In the interim, until we might move, I was treading air. I had had some doubt that getting off of Dry Fork and to Indian Creek was the change portended in my luminous vision of that spring day. I seemed not to be in a promised land yet, only in a different wilderness. But I had no doubt at all that the opening now in prospect was final fulfillment, complete and satisfying in every detail. We would live in town. I would work in a store. And I am afraid I thought of how all the Dry Fork boys would envy me.

My ecstatic vision of a rise in the world nearly faded out several times during the six weeks we remained on Indian Creek, after the rumor reached us. I think everyone forgot about it except my mother and me. After all, it was but a rumor. The intervening time had to be put in somehow. Fishing was not good after midsummer. I could not hunt squirrels, for we had no gun. I did go sometimes with an older boy, but it is of no interest to me to hunt when another does all the shooting and bags all the game.

Blackberry time came; but there were no blackberries. Another lad and I made an expedition into the bottoms in quest of woods berries. I had learned that berries may ripen in the woods when there are none to be found in the open. We filled our buckets—four quarts each—and carried them four miles to Sailor Springs where they brought us twenty cents each. The whole enterprise cost a forenoon's trudge in the bottoms of five miles, and the afternoon trip to town, another eight miles; and all for twenty cents! My mother had told me to spend half of what I received for myself.

On our dusty way to Sailor Springs my companion and I spent the dragging hour it took to walk the distance in good-natured banter. One imagined he was rich—able to drive a carriage with two horses; if he were, he would go sweeping by the other and leave him in a fog of dust. The other would see that he didn't get by; he would get a rail and thrust it into the wheels. Again, "A boy's will is the wind's will and the thoughts of youth are long, long thoughts."

I bought another pair of "store galluses" with my dime. Everything else I wore was homemade and hand-stitched, faded and worn threadbare or even fleshbare in places. But in my bright, new, elastic suspenders I felt myself perceptibly raised in the social scale. My friend wondered at all this and at my care of the dime I was taking home to my mother. He had spent his twenty cents for crackers and candy which he generously shared with me.

We had no religious contacts that summer. I do not remember that I heard any reference to God or the Bible or church or religion. A little way off was Bible Grove where there was a church. I dimly remember that some member of the family attended its services once.

There was ballad singing in that community then, as there was everywhere. To the smattering of a few folk songs we had heard on Dry Fork, we added two. One was entitled "Put My Little Shoes Away." It was the sad lament of a dying child giving instruction to its mother. Of course, no child ever did such a thing as that. But the song served its intended purpose; it made people cry.

The other song was also a doleful thing and must have had some reference to the Civil War. Even its tune had the down-

ward, minor swing and quaver of a lamentation. One stanza
had this:

> Oh, Brother Green, do come to me,
>   For I am shot and bleeding;
> Oh, tell my wife I gave my life
>   To put down this rebellion.

This song had its day of popularity. It was meant to be very
touching. It did bring tears to the eyes of the emotionally sus-
ceptible, then and there, when feelingly rendered.

During this period of waiting I had one job I could not compass—or at least did not. It was hauling haycocks from the
field with one horse and a grapevine. I could ride the horse
all right and that, finally, was the duty assigned me. But I
could not "load" the haycocks; they would "dump" and be
scattered every time. I believed that if I had had a rope instead of a grapevine and if I had been given sufficient time,
I could have done it.

It was in hay harvest that summer, when my hypothetical
good fortune was still in the balances, that Major Stanley took
a contract of putting up one hundred and fifty acres of redtop
on a farm near the little town of Rinard, some fifteen miles
from our Indian Creek location. I think Major Stanley felt
sorry for my mother in that her summer's work had paid nothing, so he proffered me the position of water boy for the dozen
hands he would require. He would pay fifty cents a day.
That was riches to us then, twice as much as I had ever been
paid. When I got up on the wagon to go with the men, my
mother stood with twitching lips, straining her eager, caressing
eyes to see the very last of me as she had done in early spring
when her older son had left her thus. When she was past
eighty, she told me that the darkest, saddest hour of her life
was that afternoon when she saw me go out into a man's world

so young. It was not a sad hour for me, as yet; I had the journey ahead.

That night I went to bed on a pallet on the rough floor of a vacant old house. As I lay there, I heard in the distance the bark of a dog that sounded just like one near us at home. I cried myself to sleep.

It rained and we had to stay there nearly three weeks, though I worked but seven days. It was a gloomy, disconsolate three weeks for me. It did not help that a bigger boy bullied me most of the time and spat tobacco juice in my eyes once when he caught me asleep.

When the hay was in stack and the owner, a Mr. Shepherd, came out from the city to pay for the work, I was chosen to drive to Rinard with an old horse and a rickety, open buggy to meet his train. There were perhaps a dozen houses in the little town but it looked like a sizable city to me. I tied my horse at the store and waited on the depot platform. When the dinkey little two-coach train came roaring and puffing in, I shrank back fearfully under the wide eaves. But the man who got off spied me and spoke, as I thought, with remarkable friendliness. He was not like any man I had ever seen. His clothes were different; his face was very smooth and fair; there was a pleasant odor about his person. He walked up to the store and went in. I followed hopefully—I knew he had money. There were many fine things in the showcases; he might wish to give me something for coming to meet him.

My passenger did not at once get into the limousine I had chauffeured in for him. He walked back and forth a time or two, filling the musty old place with the aroma of a well-groomed personality. And then he stopped where I was standing by the showcase and asked me if there was anything he could buy for me. I swallowed my heart in my excitement but managed to indicate an open purse made of black kid and lined, as I could see, with yellow. I feared lest I had made a

71

mistake; that might cost more than he wished to give me. But he smiled as he paid the twenty-five cents, and the storekeeper handed me the purse. Outside of my pocketknife and my books, I have never owned anything that meant as much to me.

I got my pay that day and crammed it all into my purse. Then I went out by myself where I could examine and gloat over my treasure.

The next day we were to go back and I would see my mother. I was wakeful but not homesick that night. We were off early, on the hayracks that had brought us. There were two teams and as many men as could ride in comfort. We would get to Flora by ten, they said. It was a gay, boisterous gang that indulged in some light, meaningless, swaggering profanity and a good deal of obscenity, meant only to raise a laugh, as I could see. I did not like it; but I was only a boy and the only boy in the gang. I thought of my mother all the way and that seemed to help some.

Flora was a railroad division point, abounding in the wildness, dissipation, and tumult common among railroad men at that time. The Flora of that day was not the same lovely city to which I was called fifty years later to conduct revival services in its leading church.

Our two hay wagons went rattling up that dusty road in a way to startle and terrify the boy holding on with both hands. The men stood up, steadying one another, yelling and shouting like a bunch of Indians as we passed the outlying houses and raising a great cloud of dust, and the wagons drew up at what seemed to be some kind of business house. The men leaped to the ground and went running in, only the drivers tarrying long enough to fasten halter straps. I followed and went in wonderingly, hindmost of them all. There was a high counter alongside and the biggest looking glass I had ever seen back of it. A big man with black mustache stood behind the counter and filled tall heavy glasses for the men to drink. One

72

of them kindly brought a glass to me and said, "Here, Sam, have some." It was a dark-looking liquid with a lot of foam on top. I did not drink it. One of the men urged me, "Drink it, Sam. It'll not hurt you—it's good." Major Stanley, himself a hard drinker, swore at the man and made him set it back on the counter; presently, as I noticed, the Major drank it himself. I asked one of the men afterward and he told me it was beer. My mother had told me about beer, but I had not seen it before. I was glad I had not tasted it, and she was glad when I told her about it that evening.

My older brother met me in Flora and we walked the six miles out in the deepening dusk of a fragrant, dewy evening in late summer. I gave my mother all the money I had earned. It helped to get us off Indian Creek and back to the little town of Geff. We had escaped from Dry Fork by way of Indian Creek.

PART II. Beginnings

Chapter 7

The Little Town of Geff

Geff had, and still has, three streets each way—north and south, east and west. Fifty years ago there were forty-four houses, three stores, two churches, a flour mill, a schoolhouse, and a post office. The branch railroad that passed through on its way from Springfield to Shawneetown had a depot far to the northwest which was moved nearer by some three squares at a later date, and then, recently, abandoned.

There were three sources of steady income in the town itself. Section men who cared for a few miles of railroad track got a dollar and five cents a day. Three schoolteachers received, all told, a total of one hundred and twenty dollars a month—forty dollars each. A dozen Civil War veterans drew pensions in varying amounts. Besides these the postmaster, the agent at the depot, and two local physicians could buy on credit at Mrs. Rapp's store if they settled the account promptly at the end of the month. Mrs. Rapp was the Dun and Bradstreet of the place. The staple money crop of farmers was redtop seed. It had a cash value and many a farmer pledged to pay "when I sell my grass seed." The sale of wheat was a factor in local economic life until chinch bugs appeared. They wintered through in wheat and became a deadly menace to corn at wheat-cutting time. Thus, because corn was the more important crop, wheat passed out of the picture. But redtop persisted and redtop time in Little Egypt was ever a season of festive doings.

This was Geff. And to us, coming from the narrow-gauge debacle at Sailor Springs, it meant again the round of ancient unpainted rented houses such as may be seen in any run-down village. We lived first in the Jeffersonville house, once a sort of hotel; then in the Miller house, just out of town; then we moved to town where we rented the Porter house, the Billy Tubbs house, and the Chick house. Then we moved to the Jesse Ward house by the mill pond; the Thorn house in town; the Milner house in the country; then, finally, back to town and the Thorn house again—nine moves in a period of six years. The highest rent we paid for any of these was three dollars a month; some were as low as a dollar, and some free.

On arrival in Geff our mother reported promptly to Mrs. Rapp and hired me out to her as chore boy about the store; it was the capsheaf of my ambition. I was to have four dollars the first month and then, in the winter, my board during the school months. The pay was small but it would help and the contact might lead to something permanent, which it did. I was twelve then and have never been out of a job since. Actually my pay was raised to five dollars a month the next spring and I stayed on there through three full years. Mrs. Rapp renamed me. I had always answered to "Sam"; she made it "Sammy," the better to fit my chubby, diminutive self, I suppose. But I never liked it, though Sammy it was in the little town of Geff forever after.

75

My first month's wage went for a ready-made suit of clothes, bought for me by my employer in Cincinnati where she went for her winter stock of goods. The suit was too large by several sizes. She bought for a twelve-year-old and I, though twelve, was of nine-year size. The fabric was shoddy, nice enough to look at though undependable for wear. But it was a step forward and I swelled with pride until I nearly filled my clothes.

I was "working in a store." I could imagine myself a young Moses marked to lead his people out of bondage and to some promised land. I did not strut when Dry Fork boys came to town, though I was conscious of a certain inward pride. As to my work, I bent to each task with a resolution not common to boys of twelve. I would do every job the very best I could. I would be cheerful and have a smile for every person I met. I would be strictly honest and truthful. I would lead in all my classes at school. We would not always be poor. One day we would be able to "buy things" like other people. I was to help toward that glad day. It was a proud ambition.

Looking back at all this secret boyish effervescence, I attribute most of it to what I had read in the dozen school readers I had gone through in the log houses of Dry Fork. The readers of that early time made much of efficiency, honor, sobriety, and industry. In spite of all I have read since about the fancies and fluctuations of adolescence, juvenile delinquency, and the ideals of youth, I do not know how that crude, freckle-faced chore boy from the back country could have done better.

The years spent in that little store stand out now, when I view them in perspective, as of far greater significance to me than any decade that has passed since. They were years of vision and unfoldment, of education in many important little things, years in a good and wholesome atmosphere. They were to me as the years Moses must have had with his mother when

76

she, as hired nurse to Pharaoh's daughter, laid in his boy's mind the spiritual foundations of his after life. Mrs. Rapp, a devout Methodist, with Puritan ideals, was as a second mother to me.

She assumed full responsibility for my bringing up, guarding me each day as she had her own son now gone away to school. Her weekly letters to him, long and detailed as they were, left an ample measure of concern for me. The store occupied one square across the street from the post office. Never a single time in the three years did I stray as far as that without a strict commission from my meticulous guardian. I have lived in many villages and have sometimes been criticized because I did not linger at stores or in the barbershop to talk. I just can't, due to that period of close surveillance by an exacting woman who knew and cared. I owe her for that, a debt that can never be paid in this world. Small-town loafing can become a passion—a corrupting passion.

There was a garden back of the store; and back of the garden an orchard; this area, three town lots in all, with barn and pigpen, was my domain. I had care of it and was wholly responsible for its appearance. But my special care was the side yard of the store which was the front yard of the three-room cottage where we ate our meals; that had to look right because everyone who passed saw it.

My experience with that yard was almost a duplicate of that related by Booker T. Washington in his *Working with the Hands*. I, too, had an uncompromising overseer; I, too, must work with a blunt-edged sickle; I, too, had to hack away hour after hour at the long tough grass to get it even. There may have been lawnmowers then, but I had never seen one. When I had finished it the first time, Mrs. Rapp came out for inspection. She made no criticism or suggestion but praised me mildly. And, to quote the words of Booker T. Washington, "When I saw that all this change and improvement was a creation of my own hands, my whole nature began to change. I felt a self-respect, an encouragement and a satisfaction that I had never before enjoyed or thought possible."

At first I slept in a room over the store, next to the one occupied by my employer. But my mother disliked for me to be away all week and asked if I might be allowed to sleep at home. This I did, and for the remainder of the three years I was on hand at the store somewhere near six o'clock, six days a week. I swept my part of the store, being directed, even to the slightest detail, until I could do it as well as the proprietress herself. That daily task of sweeping, with janitor work I presently did, made me a champion sweeper, and is one of my several skills to the present moment. How I did look forward to Sunday morning when I might sleep an extra hour or two! In due time that inclination passed. The habit of early rising, imperative six days each week, by and by covered the seventh day and I have never been able to sleep much beyond the rising hour of my boyhood.

On busy days I counted the eggs brought in; three in each hand I removed them from the customer's basket counting one, two, three with each transfer, and then dividing my count by two to get the dozens. This I marked on a slip of paper and placed in the basket. I kept my own cash box and recorded the petty sales I made so as to give a report on Saturday night. Once I was short five cents. That embarrassed me and I ransacked the whole area where my box was kept, but all in vain. Then Mrs. Rapp examined the box closely and found a "half dime" piece slipped under one edge. I hated half dimes after that and was glad when they were no longer in circulation. The store was warmed in winter with hickory wood, burned in a big box stove. I sawed the wood with a bucksaw and brought it in. We kept two pigs each autumn and I had the care of them. Old Ben, the horse, lived at a farm three miles out, save in vacation time when the son came home. Then I walked the three

78

miles and rode him in bareback. I had to ride him out again when school began and walk back to town. I fed and curried the old fellow and kept the son's buggy shining. I enjoyed all this and had no thought of complaining. Out of it all I had unappreciated gains not to be found in book or classroom.

At twenty-one the son finished his course at Lebanon. He came home then to teach in the Geff schools. He began the study of law and went to and from the county seat six miles away, so he needed a better horse. I took on the care of the new mare and the glistening new buggy with qualms. They required more careful handling. But I got on well enough, save that once when I polished the buggy wheels with a cloth moistened in kerosene, a stern and unnecessary rebuke rankled me. The young man had been brought up apart from other young people and had little regard for the lone lad from Dry Fork.

That store building, built in Civil War days, with its little cottage in the side yard, was a decided contrast to anything I had known on Dry Fork where hens and pigs often had free course to the whole residential space of the farmsteads. The old-fashioned roses, yellow and red, some of them so distractingly fragrant; the clumps of peonies and bleeding heart; the two cedar trees; the vine-shaded porch with its windlass well-curb and tincup hanging on a nail was the very gate of heaven to me then.

When my term of service came to a close I was glad of the release. I thought I might get work in the county seat, so I asked for a letter of recommendation. Mrs. Rapp assigned the task of writing it to her son. And he wrote this: "The bearer, Sammie Lappin, has worked for me over two years and I have found him an honest, hardworking boy." Rather scant and grudging, I thought. Lacking in *finesse* I might say now. I never showed it to anyone. I was rather ashamed to have worked so long for one who could not write a better commendation than that.

I cannot, in a running reminiscence like this, do justice to the woman, who, next to my own mother, had most to do with shaping my early life and directing its course. I read much in the spare hours of long summer days. Mrs. Rapp brought me from Cincinnati two books as Christmas presents. One was *Advice to Young Men* by T. S. Arthur; the other, Longfellow's *Poems* in the pearl-type edition. I read them both. I liked the poems better than the book of advice. About the store I found two volumes of *The Chatterbox* that greatly delighted me. I read them again and again. Two religious papers came weekly. They were *The Western Christian Advocate* and *The Christian at Work*. I read certain departments in both of them.

It was many years afterward that a prominent resident, passing along the street by the Rapp store building, no longer in use, pointed to the open porch and said, "There's where Sammy Lappin got his education." He did not know that I had read every readable book in his own bookcase the summer I worked for him on the farm. And the books were exactly two, *Under the Rose* by "the author of *East Lynne*," and *On the Jericho Road* by "the author of *Helen's Babies*." And he did not reckon what gains I picked up from my first lessons in two-horse farming under his somewhat impatient tutelage, nor the knowledge of human nature gathered along my huckster route later on and in a dry goods store at the county seat.

I learned very little of that small town of Geff until after I escaped from my years of benevolent incarceration. My chums and I roamed the streets on Sunday afternoons wandering far down the railroad track toward Martin Creek or into the open woods in summer. How I reveled in my new freedom! I did not have to go to the store now.

Chapter 8

Little Town Churches

There were two churches in Geff, the Methodist church across from the schoolhouse and the Christian church over to the north by the village park. They were as far apart geographically as could be if both were to be in town, and as far apart spiritually as could be if they were to be regarded as in any sense Christian. The differences most emphasized had to do with admission to the church and not with subsequent behavior. At the threshold of one stood "the good confession" voluntarily made; the other made use of the "penitent form" or "anxious seat." Baptism into the one was by immersion only, into the other by any "mode" the convert might prefer. One received the baptized convert into full membership immediately; the other required a six-month probationary period. These were the points at issue but of the three, baptism took precedence. There might be sharp firing all along the line of battle but by common consent baptism was the strong citadel to be defended by the one and assaulted by the other with all available resources.

My employer, Mrs. Rapp, had been immersed; she was neither sentimental nor combative. When Aunt Jane Stanley went into a trance during the annual revival and came out smiling and softly chanting,

"I have been in heaven, I have been in heaven,"

Mrs. Rapp said, "Well, Jane, if you want my opinion, you'd better have stayed there."

I heard her say once to a presiding elder, "I've never felt like shouting, but a time or two I've reached the point where everything around me looked as bright as a dollar." I thought that a rather good testimony, for a dollar looked pretty bright to her.

I attended the Christian church after beginning my work in the village store. Mrs. Rapp approved, as I afterward learned; she thought a boy ought to go with his mother. When I was offered the janitorship of the church that summer, she generously granted me time off to attend to my new duties. The pay was a dollar and a half a month, which, added to the five dollars she paid me, as may be readily calculated, gave me the rather handsome income of seventy-eight dollars a year. My older brother was then earning a little over three hundred a year and my sister had occasional employment in families at fifty cents a week. We were subsisting, the five of us, on a good deal less than five hundred dollars a year. But, by comparison with our Dry Fork situation, we were rolling in wealth. We had "arrived," or at least we thought we had. We lived in frame houses now—no more log cabins. We were in school—a school near at hand, no more long weary trudging over muddy or frozen roads in clothing all too scant. We had come to town. Best of all, to my mother's way of thinking, we were near a church.

And such a church it was! The frame building was commodious, always cold in winter and always warm in summer. It was never ventilated, for I was the janitor and the sashes were too hard for me to move, either up or down.

Even less attractive than the house were the public services. We began late, for time is unimportant to little-town people with no streetcars to meet, no whistles to blow, no time clocks to punch. Our church finances were always a drag. We had preaching once a month part of the time, by whoever happened in. We tolerated factionalism and petty quarrels over inconsequential matters and granted undue consideration to the principals. We did all that could be done, humanly speaking, to kill that church. But it did not die. The powers of the unseen world, so dominant in Geff at that time, did not prevail against it.

That church was better than anything we had ever known. It was the very gate of heaven to our hungry souls. And with one possible exception—the Methodist church—it was the best thing in Geff.

I joined the Christian church over by the park at thirteen. I was janitor at fourteen, deacon and Sunday school teacher at sixteen, and was ordained to the ministry there at twenty-two. Our church had in it one man, Wat Bestow, who, though never quite sympathetic and helpful to a boy, nevertheless did much for me in one way and another. For many traits that seem to have been bred in him, I did not like him at all; but I loved him and love him still, for his unceasing service in the little church where I was born anew.

Since I was the janitor, I had to be there at every service; I was paid to be there—paid more or less regularly, less than fifty cents a week. Often I was the "only man there." And there was a smoldering sentiment to the effect that a woman must not be heard in a public service. She might respond if asked to have part in the meeting or she might ask a question from the pew, but it took a masculine mind to lead!

On a certain evening in early summer when June bugs were at the worst, the five or six women present prevailed upon me to lead the meeting. I did my best, read at a venture, for I scarcely knew one Testament from the other, and muttered something meant to be a prayer when those present stood for the last stanza of a song. The women did the rest. The next day a resident local preacher said with pleased astonishment,

"It never was heard of for a fourteen-year-old boy to lead a prayer meeting—that boy ought to be a preacher!" I heard what he had said and the remark may have given direction to my wishful thinking.

However, that man, though my father in the gospel, was not wholly responsible for thus encouraging a mere neophite to enter the sacred calling. Others than he were implicated, mainly one other.

There came to our church about that time a man named John Williams. We had two factions in the church—and the wrong faction invited Williams to come. That gave him a bad start. But after the first discourse everybody knew a different kind of preacher had come to town. He preached above the factional level. He was a sort of universal, ecumenical Christian. We had heard no preacher like him. Clear, tender, and appealing were his private counsels and his gracious public exhortations. His coming healed much of our petty partisanship. Our Methodist neighbors attended and helped with a few fervent amens. Thoughtful outsiders expressed approval by being present in numbers.

My mother was a good judge of preaching. One evening after the service, as I led her up the quiet moonlit street to our little home, she gripped my arm with firm hand and said, her voice vibrant with suppressed emotion, "Sam, I would rather hear you preach one sermon like the one Brother Williams preached tonight than to see you President of the United States." John Williams and my mother had their part in making me a preacher.

Then came Brother Henessee to that Methodist circuit. I saw him, his girl wife at his side, as I peered out from behind a pile of muslin, where Mrs. Rapp greeted the newly arrived minister of her church beamingly. He could not have been much past twenty-two and his wife, seemingly, was younger still. My heart went out to them. I liked them both because they were young.

My mother's little house was across the road from the barn of the Methodist parsonage. By accident I discovered that the young minister rehearsed his sermons at the barn on the evening he was to preach at Geff. Clandestinely, I stole out there at each practice period and listened, with only an oak board between me and the young preacher. I enjoyed that experience greatly and would usually steal round to the church to hear how the sermon went off.

I remember a night in November when I stood in a thick mist listening and something new occurred. The sermon had a stanza or two of poetry and somehow my friend could not get by that part. I think I tried agonizingly to help him with it, but even the two of us could not get past that trouble spot. Presently he gave it up and was silent. I thought he had stolen out. Then I heard a movement in the hay and he was speaking again in a different and much subdued tone. He was praying. He asked God to help him make it a good sermon even if he had to omit the poetry. I felt as if I had intruded into the Holy of holies. I got away as softly as I could. Then I sat in the church waiting until he came. It was a slim hearing he would have. A dozen or so had straggled into the dim, lamplighted room and were seated about the one stove. The air was stale and smelled of sauerkraut. The few lamps that had been lighted had smoky chimneys. Boys were whispering loudly. The saints sat waiting, Mrs. Rapp central among them, warmly wrapped in her big dolman cloak, the black fascinator of that day about her head and neck, reverent, dignified, and in deep meditation, as was fit. I looked about restlessly, waited and wondered.

Presently my friend, the young preacher, came in. He went slowly up the aisle and was seated on the front pew of the "amen corner." I watched him closely. He cast a look about

85

now and then, as if to discover who else had come. The door latch clicked a time or two as latecomers entered. Ruben McCoy, the bewhiskered janitor, made loud noises at the big wood-burning stove. The organist fluttered the leaves of a songbook. Rain dashed against the windows and an autumn wind added its dirgelike accompaniment to all as if to give final touch and tone to the bleak, odorous dreariness. Then the young preacher looked back over his dumb, disinterested auditory, laid back the overcoat from his shoulders, lifted his face heavenward, cleared his voice, and began to sing. He had a good tenor voice. His song was new to us. I have sung it as best I could through the years and sing it still, and never do I sing a strain of it that I do not see that young man, sole champion of God and his gospel, in that sweltering moral mud-hole, trying to lift himself and his parishioners out by the boot-straps of his own faith and optimism:

> My Father is rich in houses and lands,
> He holdeth the wealth of the world in his hands;
> Of rubies and diamonds, of silver and gold,
> His coffers are full—he has riches untold.
>
> A tent or a cottage, why should I care,
> They're building a mansion for me over there,
> Though exiled from home, yet still will I sing,
> "With Jesus my Savior, I'm the child of a king."

Through seventeen years of service in the village and country churches of Illinois I lifted myself out of desperate situations by singing that song in memory of Brother Henessee, youthful Methodist rider on the Geff circuit.

Other Christian preachers came—Johnson, Morris, Taylor, Tait, Manker. Most of them were teachers mainly, using charts and maps and giving some insight into the Bible, dates, divisions, and geographical setting. Tait was a preacher and

86

a good preacher. Manker was my favorite. He made wise appeal to the emotions. He would labor some twenty or thirty minutes to make the way of the Christian life plain; then, with all the fervor and persuasiveness of his warm, affectionate nature, he would urge his hearers to enlist publicly for the new and better life. That sort of evangelism appealed to me. It still does.

An event of note in my memory of the religious life of the little town is the Hill-Spence-McMinn revival. It began, modestly enough, in the Methodist church as I now recall, and broadened into a community affair. It followed the lines of the union meeting that had its innings not long afterward; but the technique had not been worked out as in the day of J. Wilbur Chapman, Billy Sunday, William E. Biederwolf, Charles R. Scoville, and Billy Graham.

Hill was preacher at the first. Slight of build, nervous, pale almost to whiteness, he was active, warmly fervent, and had a voice of some compass, capable of expressing emotion. Spence was the singer; preacher and singer teams were new then. McMinn, a Baptist who was better known locally than either of the other two, gradually swung into stride and took precedence as an evangelistic preacher. When crowds outgrew the church building, a large tent was brought in and, with lumber from nearby sawmills, seats and platform were built. That added impetus and interest. Everybody attended. Religion was the main issue in any small community then.

Many converts were made. Many church members hungered to be made over spiritually, so some sort of second blessing or reconsecration was held up as remedy for halting faith. The neighbors entertained the ministering brethren. More than once Hill was a dinner guest at the cottage by the store and in the interim between the noonday meal and the afternoon service I would listen to the confident expoundings of the evangelist. Mrs. Rapp hung with undivided interest and evident admiration on his every word. I do not think she understood much of it, I am sure I did not. It seemed to me that sonorous words and tones and an occasional "oratorical pause" were made a substitute for clearness and good sense. But to Mrs. Rapp he was a holy man and could do no wrong.

One example of what was called "the work of the Holy Spirit" gives me cold shivers even now. A farmer I knew well, who lived three miles west of town (in the direction of Dry Fork), attended the meeting night after night and became emotionally stirred. He was of the type that, in the revivals of that day, exhibited what was thought to be spiritual and significant manifestations in a high degree. One night after rocking to and fro in a sitting posture on the platform, singing and shouting, this man suddenly broke into a fit of uncontrollable laughter. His performance held the center of the stage. They could not stop him or "sing him down." After an hour or two when most of the people had gone home, his friends loaded him bodily into an open buggy to get him away. Until the tent lights were out and the last stragglers homeward bound, his demoniacal laughter could be heard receding slowly as the old horse towed him toward home. The memory of his strange, wild gales of mirthless laughter, one outburst after another mingled with the song most used,

Are you washed in the blood,
In the soul-cleansing blood of the Lamb,

is a fearsome thing to me even now. That man, and three others most wrought upon in the after-meeting excesses, died in later life as they themselves feared, without God and without hope. They had never caught any slight impression of the blessings assured in the gospel or of the life Christians ought to live. But that was a "great revival," i.e., the team was well paid.

Neither of the local churches was much involved in the meetings. It was an invasion from the outside, as such meetings usually are. Certain impressionable individuals, not the most thoughtful and considerate, took hold and lent such influence as their presence and the noise they might make could supply. They were of those who love publicity such as only emotional revivals offer. My two friends, Mrs. Rapp of the Methodist church and Elder Bestow of the Christian church, were not often seen about the tent; neither were they heard to offer criticism. It was to them a celestial medicine show under religious auspices. Both, as I now see it, regretted the excesses and foresaw the results that would follow. It is my conviction that the revival did harm to Christianity. It was the rude forerunner of "union evangelism" that swept the field *ad nauseum* three generations later. Sam Jones of Georgia was even then creating sensation in the cities with his bald, blunt attacks on sin and the hypodermic needles of his incisive wit. Billy Sunday and now Billy Graham lifted the method to a higher level.

It is one thing to be near a church, convenient to religious services, and quite another to take full advantage of it all and get in the game—to help things along and to be helped by helping others. Many influences keep good people—especially young people—from getting full value from religious worship. Occupations may hinder; rigorous employment during the week that make a day of absolute rest and relaxation imperative. Or it may be the lack, or imagined lack, of suitable clothes to wear or the human tendency that is in us all, to take the way of least resistance or greatest present attractiveness.

My older brother had no church leanings. Something along the way had estranged him. He was not merely indifferent at this period; he was slightly antagonistic. It may have been the talk he had heard from men in his knocking about among those untouched by any influence from another level.

Our mother saw this, I am sure, and regretted it, but she

89

did not have the heart to insist or press her wishes on him. On Dry Fork it had been a rule that we were not to go fishing on Sunday. But, now, when he must work six days, that rule was relaxed in his case and on a certain Sunday he could go to Deer Creek to fish. But that projected a problem for my mother. If he might go, why not I also? I liked fishing as well as he and I, too, worked six days each week. But I was janitor of the church. It was finally arranged that if I could get a substitute I might go along. I had the tackle in shape and a bountiful can of worms so we could be off early. Away we went, "our cares behind, our hearts ahead," up the railroad track to Deer Creek.

When I was well settled atop a flat stump, my hook baited with a worm I felt sure would have catfish appeal, and had chosen a particular opening in the lily pads near a drift, I heard the mellow tones of the church bell three miles distant! The Bible school would be assembling and I would not be there. And I was a member of the church! I do not think it was the guilt of fishing on Sunday that smote me that day nor the wrong of being where I was, so much as of *not being where I knew I ought to be.* I was not happy and our fishing trip was a failure. I have never baited a hook on Sunday since that day. I think I understand the mood of the group on Galilee that at dawn must say to the great Fisherman, "Master, we toiled all night and took nothing!" That strikes me as about the most accurate, perhaps the only really true, fish story on record.

My brother softened in his attitude toward the church as we were one by one gathered in. He learned to know the little town and its corrupting influences though they never touched him. He was always a sober, industrious man. When he had worked for a long time in the West as farm hand, as cow puncher, as pioneer claimant of public land, as railroad employee, an evangelist who knew me was called to conduct services in the Colorado town where my brother was living. One day I received a special delivery letter stating that my brother was attending the meetings night after night and that a letter from me might prompt him to make public profession. I took as much pains with that letter as with any I have ever written. Before many days had passed, word came to me that he had united with the church. "It looked this way to me, Sam," he said, when we met again, "a man takes no chances in joining the church. If everything is as we have been taught to believe, he's on the safe side; but even if it is not, he has had the best there is in this life."

Going to church services regularly every Lord's Day is not a source of deep satisfaction native to the average boy. It was not to me. I knew I ought to go, but often I was conscious of other places I would rather have gone. I sat by a window many a Lord's Day in winter and eyed the rabbit tracks that stole out from under the meetinghouse, through the fence and across Wat Bestow's orchard, and wished I might be out there in the snow pursuing him. Or in summer when lads I knew came from behind Henry Jamison's barn and held up two fingers tauntingly at me, I knew they were off to Sheep Ford for a swim. But today, when the years have flown, though the rabbits still track the snow around the church at night and the boys still go swimming (or wish they might) on Sunday forenoons, I am glad I stayed with the church. I know the subsequent history of every Geff boy of that generation, and I know my own full well. The church way was the right way; it was my only way out. All that is as clear to me as a demonstration in geometry.

It was nearly fifty years later that three of us, the Lappin brothers, returned to the little old town for a season of summer evangelism. I went from Pittsburgh, with two hundred and fifty dollars in my pocket to see the thing through, one of the twins from a preacher training school in Tennessee, and

91

the other from a university in Oklahoma. We joined forces, a musical combination as our aid, in a great tent in the park by the village hall. Gaping neighbors wondered dumbly at the preparations that were being made. One said, as the tent was being spread, "If all the people in Geff turned out, the tent would not be half full." But delegations came from a radius of a hundred miles. Crowds ranging from three hundred to three thousand thronged the park daily. It was a unique incident. The chance product of one generation was seeking to bridge over to another generation further on and to leave there something of what had been learned from the outside world. The enterprise paid out in full, so that not a dollar of what I had brought had to be spent. It was during the great depression, too. The event is still part of the unwritten history of the little town, retold sometimes by village folk loitering in the barber shop or in front of the filling station where the two roads cross and along one of which, now, a steady procession of traffic courses day by day, and far into the night, the whole year through.

Across the street, northward from the little village park, stands the story-and-a-half house where once lived the Bestow family, prominent then in the local aristocracy. About that house cluster the sentiments and legends most apt to be recalled by those who return on homecoming occasions.

Central in the scene, as I recall it, stands always the figure of that robust, voluble, intensely human personality that dominated it in the days of my youth, Waterman Bestow, ruling elder in the church that did so much for me. What he and the church meant to me in the time of my metamorphosis I could not tell by spoken word or written page. If I could, it would be but the story of ten thousand such standing guard, spiritually, in the little towns and remote rural regions of America, sometimes battling valorously against "spiritual wickedness in high places."

Chapter 9

School Life in the Little Towns

Two doors, and only two, were open to the wide-eyed, wondering group of orphans who drifted into Geff from the Ozarks by way of Dry Fork and Indian Creek. They were the schoolhouse door and the church door. We tried the schoolhouse first; we felt sure of an unconditional welcome there. We imagined that cleaner faces, better clothes, and more refined behavior would be expected at the church.

Four of us, for the twins were of school age now, reported on the first day, and were assigned to classes. How strange it was to us—that big schoolhouse, with its three rooms, primary, intermediate, and "upstairs" all under one roof, with the Masonic hall using half of the second story to make up the cubical structure. We had known only the little dry-goods box of a house in the woods, with its four windows on a side and its barren lack of all comfort or embellishment.

Again I was afraid. A paralyzing sense of inferiority, born of backwoods oblivion, returned and gripped me. The boys who had bullied me when I rode Old Charley to town with a grist of corn would be there. Other boys and girls who lived in "frame houses" and had carpets on their floors would be there. I had no knowledge of who the teachers were or what they might be like. I was a poor boy, unknown to any save as "Mrs. Rapp's chore boy."

I climbed the stairs with heavy, hesitant tread. I tried to be furtive and quiet so as not to attract the attention of anyone. Reluctantly and scared, I turned into the room, half filled now with chattering youngsters of my own age or older, but all much larger than I. Near the door and at one side stood the new teacher greeting his pupils of the first day. I had one look at that beaming face. It was the kindliest and most encouraging human visage I had ever seen. His touch, as with others I filed by, thrilled me. The memory of that first week, when we were getting acquainted, has lost nothing of its warm glow in the years that intervene.

I carried in my heart a heavy burden all that year—a burden I have never mentioned until now. I was sharing a good home. I had enough good food at each meal. I slept in a featherbed (that first year) and in a newly whitewashed room. No other members of my family fared as well; and my elder brother, who should have been in school, was out on the right-of-way, blown by wintry winds, baked by summer suns, doing the work of a man when but eighteen. In addition, he had nothing for himself out of what he earned; he was our bread-winner. I was envied by some of the boys I came to know, and regarded as very fortunate by older folk who congratulated me on having so good a home. But that was not my home. Others of my family were living in little rented houses here and there, carried about by circumstance, less fortunate by far than I.

It was a thrice-welcome change to me when I was granted leave to sleep at home, though it meant giving up the warm featherbed and a room to myself for a "straw tick" shared by my older brother. But, insignificant as was the change, it kept the family whole and preserved a tender fellowship—a fellowship that neither time, change, distance, circumstances, nor death has ever marred.

James H. Kramer came to teach in the Geff schools the year I entered there. Since my mother led me by the hand up a briar-grown Missouri hillside on a day in May seven years before, I had known no man capable of appreciating and assisting a fatherless boy. This man did, and I willingly paid him the homage that only an eager and hungry-hearted lad can bestow.

Our teacher sought to understand his pupils and to be understood by them. They and he were friends. His was not the mere obligation to teach, as I at once understood; it was privilege—the privilege of seeing to it that young life got off to a fair start. What he had for us was not contained chiefly in books; he sought by every possible contact and with sincere educational passion to pour the treasures of his own consecrated life into our rustic, awestruck, and often unwilling bosoms. He had something in the way of qualification to teach that I have never discerned in any other person. With all his passionate enthusiasm he sought to bridge the space between the best he himself had shared and the dumb intellectual poverty of our little town.

Mr. Kramer was supposed to have supervising control over the two lower rooms. I observed that he did not supervise at all; he visited the other teachers, fraternized with them, eyed the exercises displayed on blackboards, fluttered the leaves of torn textbooks, glanced at the roster of names, and patted the younger boys and girls on their heads. By irresistible good fellowship he got others to do what needed to be done without even making a suggestion.

This teacher of ours was a member of the Methodist Episcopal Church. I did not know this at first. Our two little churches indulged in no mutual admiration gestures. The nastiest antagonism in the little town was that between them. As janitor of one I presumed to carry an undue responsibility as its defender. I entertained secret but serious doubts about the salvation of anyone in the Methodist Church save my employer, Mrs. Rapp. I made exception in her case. When I learned that Mr. Kramer was a Methodist, I was somewhat set back. I would have to let him pass, too. And it seeped into my religious consciousness presently that, after all, it is the Christ in us and not the denomination with which we hold membership that counts. My teacher revealed this to me without himself knowing that he did it.

To every recitation he brought a sort of human interest I have never known to attend the work of any other instructor. We saw the characters of history; he made us see them. The celebrities of literature had communion with us as we drank in their charmed words and phrases. The pageantry of ages unrolled before us. Best of all a high moral cast was given to what we heard and said and did in school hours.

It comes to me now, as a bright vision, sweet to recall, how he used to have those who would do so remain for an hour after school while he read to us out of classics of which we never had heard. In that way we became acquainted with *The Hoosier Schoolmaster,* "Snow Bound," *Evangeline,* "Hiawatha," and "Gray's Elegy Written in a Country Churchyard." Long, long afterward I visited Stoke Pogis Church on an afternoon in spring and there purchased a memorial copy of the Elegy.

That school term brought in and held many from the far corners of the district. But Mr. Kramer yearned for more. Several of the older boys had quit school a year or two before. The teacher sought out all of these, called on them in their homes, and formed separate classes so that they might make up for lost time. Once or twice a week he conducted a writing school at night and sought to improve us beyond what was possible in school hours. His was truly a consuming zeal. It was when he was reading the Elegy to us that a significant thing took place. He read with genuine feeling the great passages and often paused to comment on some phrase or stanza. On a day when but a dozen of us were present, he had read with tremulous overtone the seven or eight stanzas until he came to this,

The boast of heraldry, the pomp of power.

Something unusual in his faltering expression at that point caught the interest of us all. When he came to the closing lines of that verse,

And all that beauty, all that wealth e'er gave,
Await alike th' inevitable hour:—

he went on, deeply moved, to read:

The paths of glory. . . .

and, choking with emotion, could barely get through with the words,

lead but to the grave.

He closed the book and said brokenly, "That is all for today— you are excused." We left the room silently and outside one of the older boys said in hushed voice, "You know his father just died." We were enrolled in the school of life.

We had some rowdy boys. There had to be a showdown in discipline. One tough youth of good family—the one who had twitted my sister and me about the oyster cans—was the center of most of the unrest. Mr. Kramer watched him; he cultivated him as much as he could an insolent chap of that type. However, the bold young ruffian was resentful of all hints at restraint. But there came a day. . . . One day, before the forenoon recess, the principal asked us to be more quiet going down the stairs so as not to disturb those below. Then he stood at the door. Along came the recalcitrant one and down he went as usual, three steps at a time, making a thunderous noise with calfskin boots. To his utter astonishment the agile Mr. Kramer was there when he landed and back up they went, the offender pale at the gills. Such a going over as that big boy got none of us gaping and dumbfounded younger ones had ever heard. There was not a touch of physical correction—just a complete, verbal barrage that nearly paralyzed us all. The whole school trembled, but silently approved.

The boy was never the same after that; he became a model of deferential regard and good behavior. I recall a day when it appeared that Dick Black and Elbie Blackburn were about to come to blows on the playground. The chastened rowdy rushed in and stood between them, pleading with evident sincerity,

"Look here, you fellows, listen to me; for goodness' sake, don't stir him up again; once is enough for this term."

I stood in awe of the big boys of the school that winter. They were a rugged, raucous, tough bunch—good humored, to be sure, but youthful ruffians proud of their physical prowess. After school, on my way from the store to the post office to get the mail as I had to do daily, I would pass a group of them at a favorite loitering place. In due time we came to an understanding and were good fellows together. I was spared their usual rough treatment on account of my size; but one of them made it a practice to lay hold of me and search my pockets for a chance bit of candy he thought might be there. I broke him of that. My employer allowed me to look after the candy shelf, even suggesting that I take a bite now and then if I cared to, as, of course, I often did. A favorite confection then was a ball of candied coconut, so, counseling no one, I opened a coconut ball and deposited a goodly portion of cayenne pepper inside, closing it neatly again. Thus armed, I invaded that rowdy bunch several evenings before my beefy assailant repeated his stunt. And when he did, he was then and thereafter a laugh-

ingstock among his fellows. His favorite act was never repeated. And we were friends until his demise in midlife.

Most teachers, as alert pupils soon find out, lay particular
emphasis on certain features of school life. Some things are
forbidden; others are compulsory; boys and girls must fit themselves to a particular mold or schedule. There must be no whispering. There may be Bible reading—at least it was so then.
Handwriting or mathematics or grammar will be the main issue.

Mr. Kramer was different. He turned his boys and girls
loose, indicated the several fields of learning to be explored, en-
couraged us as we began, and all along the way took notice of
our progress and bestowed due praise. He said nothing about
religion but took the two churches for granted and paid deference to both. He laid down no rules but lived before us a radiant and gladsome life. We were not curbed or shut in at any
point but the particular expression of his face gave approval
or suggested dissent plainly enough to be understood by all. We
were guided as by a radio beam—the beam of his approving
eye. I think we learned from him things he did not himself
know! I believe now that he was a student along with us of
some things covered in that strange and expanding school.

Mr. Kramer taught us for one term of five months. For
that service he was paid three hundred dollars—sixty dollars a
month. Then he was elected county school superintendent and
another teacher came. At the end of that second term of five
months a dozen of us went to the county seat to take the examination for second-grade teacher's license. We were examined
in "the seven branches." I went by invitation as a sort of mascot, the runt of the bunch; I was but sixteen years old. It was
the impetus gained during Mr. Kramer's winter term that carried us this far. Perhaps the fact that he would be the examiner
was an added inducement. All but three of us were passed,
some by grace, no doubt. I attained the grades, but was not old

enough since seventeen years was the minimum for teachers. I counted myself a charity case, passed by good will.

However, I would be old enough to teach next year if I could get a school, so I began my quest over muddy roads on foot, in early spring. I walked twenty miles—across Dry Fork and on into Hickory Hill. I canvassed half a dozen schools, walking over unbelievable roads to interview bristly-faced directors, and to be questioned narrowly and surveyed by their none-too-considerate eyes. Later the report filtered back to Geff that Tom Thumb had been out that way applying for schools.

It was on this unsuccessful tour that I stayed overnight in the home of a woodsman who was boarding several tiemakers. By trading around I had come into possession of a unique sort of pocketknife. It was a toy more than a knife, I had discovered, a mere novelty. One of the men caught sight of it, asked for it, and examined it curiously. He asked me what I would take for it—would I take fifty cents? I would and did, cash on the spot. I had not possessed that much money in months. Before I slept, I decided what I would do with it. I set out for home early next day; it took some hours to traverse twenty miles of slush and mud on foot. I arrived at the little house in Geff in the middle of the afternoon. I rested a while and then told my mother about the sale of my knife and said that I was going out to John McFeeley's to get salt pork. To my surprise it hurt her deeply. She knew how I valued a pocketknife. But it was winter and we needed fats and protein food which we had lacked almost wholly for weeks. I have never cared for salt pork but that particular meat was good. During that period of economic stress we were communistic—like the church at Jerusalem— in that no one said that aught he possessed was his own.

I did not get a school that year, but my sister, two years older, did, and that helped at home. Our total income had no significance to any individual of us. The family possessions were administered for the benefit of all. It was "Ours for us, not mine for me."

I sallied forth earlier next year, but tragically there was a change in the law and one must be eighteen to teach. Besides my gradings, that were valid for one year only, would expire; I would have had to be re-examined anyway. My chum and I hit upon a ruse; we wrote Mr. Kramer and asked for the courtesy of a private examination, just before the new law came into effect. We passed and were qualified to teach when the law changed and no man could say us nay, though we were but seventeen.

I needed a job for the summer. A new farmer from Randolph County, Indiana, had bought Maple Crossing Farm, halfway between Geff and the county seat. He offered me twelve dollars a month if I would work for him five months. I accepted and raced home to assure my mother that we would still have bread.

My employer was away a good deal. He would talk with me about the farm and indicate what work lay ahead. I managed it myself and got all the work done, with time for certain minor repairs needed about the barn and garden. That is the way I like to work. I was never able to do my best if someone stood by telling me what and how. That was a great summer for me. I began to grow. That transforming change was at hand when glands let loose the magic hormones in the human body. My arms and legs lengthened a little, my muscles hardened, my thorax enlarged and deepened. I developed into a man— not much of a man, to be sure, for I kept on growing until I was twenty-two to attain even average stature.

I got a school that autumn. My employer on the farm was chosen school director and with his help I was given Pleasant Hill School at eighteen dollars a month! I admit I had pull. I "used influence," agreeing to board with one of the directors at a dollar and a quarter a week. But I had a school at last;

we were arriving; we would be able sometime to buy things like other people.

The last day of school was an occasion then. I had my mind on that community event from the first day on. I entertained a hope that by that time I might get a new ready-made suit. There were two clothiers in the county seat, one a long-established merchant, the other newly come. I went to the first-named, for I had been in his store often. I told him I wished to get a twelve-dollar suit to be paid for when my school was out. He asked me the names of my directors; and at that moment one of them, a businessman of the town, came riding by on horseback. The merchant accosted him and asked if he would guarantee the account. He refused, so that was that. I thought he ought to have done so, but I did not much blame him. How could he know that a young sprout like me would pay his debts?

I went to the other store, the new man in town. He received me cordially, "Why, of course, Mr. Laffin" (he called me Laffin for years), "of course you can get a suit here." I paid the bill promptly and I bought many suits there afterward. I counted him my good friend for many years.

I did not lose touch with Kramer. At the end of his service as county school superintendent he went into the lumber business. I was secretly grieved at this, almost outraged; but I did not blame him. No man could make a living teaching school then, with salaries what they were. But I felt that a pedagogical genius was being lost to the teaching profession when Kramer quit.

Chapter 10

Schools and Schoolteaching

The roads by which aspiring youth might get out of Little Egypt were not many. Schoolteaching, preaching, politics, and the study of law were the ones oftenest chosen. Some tried more than one of these before finding exit; others tried them all and were still in bondage; the greater part tried none of them but were content to stay around the old haunts and go twice a day to the depot to see the trains come in, or in outlying regions, to go coon-hunting on Saturday nights in winter and fishing in summer.

Senators Borah and Jones took to law and politics. Dr. Ira W. Howerth, after teaching a few terms, read law and then made final choice of the teaching profession. My boyhood teacher and friend, J. H. Kramer, went into a successful business career by way of teaching and politics. There are always means within reach by which the fittest can survive.

For most of us the schoolteacher and preacher seemed to be the only ones who dressed well, had the respect of all, and got their money without physical labor. The eyes of eager youth are not slow in discerning these things. And it was this, I am persuaded, that often led to decision. I doubt if many of us had any real passion for pedagogy or if any felt, with the Apostle, "Woe is unto me, if I preach not the gospel!" Rather there was an inner and unconscious conviction to the effect that "Woe is me if I don't find some way to buy good clothes and get out of Little Egypt." Schoolteaching was the easiest and most accessible path open to us.

However, I was not to be a teacher. I did not know enough, and what I knew lacked the preciseness and accuracy essential to effective teaching. I knew enough things but they were not the right things and I did not know them well enough. But even if the way had been open for me to qualify more fully, I would not have been a successful teacher. I was in too much of a hurry; I required a more active life and a more varied outlook than was to be had from the schoolroom of that day. Besides I did not wish to be a teacher. I had noticed that many of those who stay in the profession tire of acquiring new knowledge, go in a circle, and cease to grow.

Yet I had a passion to teach school and enjoyed it, but only as an approach to something else—an escape, as it were. Dealing with human nature in the rough always fascinated me. But I craved association with adults who knew more than I, not with children who knew less. I taught school and liked it because I had to.

Five months at Pleasant Hill with twenty-four pupils in eight grades and an income of only eighteen dollars a month did not give me much of a start. But at least I had got beyond Tom Thumb proportions. I could approach unfeeling directors with better grace. I had had experience.

I scouted the county over that year from early spring, seeking a school, but without success or encouraging prospect. Teachers were made to beg for schools then. Each of three directors had to be visited and persuaded or otherwise influenced.

Important as it was that I get a school, I could not give all my time to the quest. I had to make a living for myself and part of my family. I hired out to a local storekeeper to drive his huckster wagon through the country, trading dry goods and notions for country produce. That experience was not without benefit to me. Therein also was education, and I was but eighteen. I had to manage my mule team and to get my ponderous old peddling wagon over impossible, unimproved roads. I had to get acquainted with new people and make them like me. I had to calculate values, and extend limited credit to those I judged to be good pay.

In midsummer I was called off this job and sent to an adjoining county to take charge of a stock of merchandise my employer had acquired. Through long, summer days in that remote, crossroads store I took to writing for country papers— essays, news items, screeds, even verses. A few of them were published. I had always enjoyed putting my thoughts down on paper. It was the summer of the Johnstown flood. I composed a long poem on "The Hero of Conemaugh," but if it ever attained to more than mere national notice I have not heard of it—really, though, I have not traveled abroad very much.

In the late summer I returned home. It was nearly autumn when I set about finding a school. We four had to live somehow. Looking back, I wonder I did not get the jitters. I would now. Often there was not a whole dollar between us and insolvency, though we had always our just quota of credit at the village stores. Everybody knew the Lappins were poor but nobody doubted that they were honest and would pay.

I heard of a school nine miles away on upper Dry Fork that had not yet hired a teacher. I borrowed a horse from my chum's father, an itinerant preacher, and rode the distance, arriving at noon the day decisions were to be made. I stayed right on the job and got the school. But there was a circumstance connected with the deal that pained me.

The only other applicant was a man who had not done well at farming and had turned to his studies again to qualify for teaching. He had attended the county teachers' institute and received his certificate. He had a wife and two young children. He was a good fellow, too, as I quickly discovered while we sat on a log outside Old Salem Church waiting until the three directors had deliberated within.

One of the directors came out presently and announced that I had been given the school. My heart bounded with joy; but when I saw the other candidate mount his horse and ride gloomily away, I was smitten with remorse. He was older than I, had his little family to support, and wanted that school most fervently. I wished sincerely that I could decline in his favor. But I, too, was the only support of a family of four; my sister had married and my older brother had gone West at twenty-one to take up a claim.

I pocketed my contract and set out for home at sunset. I was eager to let my mother know before she slept that we would have an income of thirty dollars a month for the winter. Our home that summer was in one of the long unused houses of an earlier era, located in an old orchard back from the public road two miles west of Geff. I planned to return the pony to its owner that night. But I decided to ride home first to report the good news, and then go on to town. I could walk back, as I calculated, by midnight.

We galloped most of the way home and arrived at that ancient farmhouse and neglected old orchard at about ten o'clock. No one was at home—a thing quite unusual. I found a window open and got in. Everything was in order. Evidently my mother and the twins had gone to some neighbor's for the night. I decided to stay and return my borrowed horse next morning. I was up and off at daylight and back on foot by nine o'clock.

Needless to say my mother was relieved when I arrived and announced that I had a school for the winter. Then, when we two were alone, my mother told me that the night before, she had thought she would die from sheer loneliness if she stayed another night in that desolate place, not knowing where I was; and how, returning in the morning and finding that I had come and gone, such a sense of unutterable misery came over her that she wished she might die. But she had calculated my movements correctly and was preparing our frugal noonday meal when I arrived. "I knew you would come," she said. The *pièce de résistance* of that meal, as often happened at our table, was strong black coffee. The sun shone out that day with exceptional brightness.

We moved back to town to the Thorne house. We got along somehow until my school began a month later. Our credit at the stores was not strained though it might be a matter of nine weeks before any sure money would come our way. I had to meet that economic crisis somehow, so I went to each merchant in our little town and inquired as to what we owed. This I set down in a little blank book I have kept until now. Then I told each one we owed that I would be teaching Watson School for the winter and would take care of the account as soon as possible after school began. This was perfectly satisfactory. Each one seemed pleased to grant an extension. We got through the late summer on garden stuff; I earned an honest half dollar now and then tamping redtop seed at the warehouses; the twins earned their share at sundry chores for the neighbors. Then each month, when I had my thirty dollars, I paid a third on each account until all was paid. I have found that nearly any creditor will be reasonable when honest intention is shown.

My schoolteaching experience took on a variety of features that winter. I had to walk the nine miles to and from the community each week—that or miss being at home for the week end; and I did not miss a single time. I boarded and roomed at a farmhouse for ten cents a meal with no charge for the room. My school consisted of eight grades and more; that is, there were some who pursued studies beyond the eight grades then customary in rural schools. I taught a class in advanced arithmetic and one or two students did individual reading under my direction, with me keeping ahead, pioneering into fields not before explored by me.

One of the older boys had a brother, a teacher in an adjoining district, who secretly induced him to request me to have a class in algebra. I knew my neighbor well enough to understand the intrigue; he wished me to expose the fact that I had not studied algebra, as he had, just a little. I rose to the occasion and defeated his ruse with much glory to myself. I said, "Of course; let us have a class in algebra; we can find time for it someway, even if we have to stay after school hours."

I asked them to secure textbooks and bring them the next Monday. They brought them but only two were alike. I delayed the class a week and committed to memory ten pages of algebra. The books were alike that far, I soon found. Presently we had suitable books and were ready to go, so I assigned a liberal first lesson. Our initial recitation was ideal. The two boys and four girls, all older and larger than their teacher, were good sports; they made a fine showing. I stressed the necessity of getting the first pages thoroughly and gave them a longer lesson. Each night I betook myself to the cold bedroom with my dim kerosene lamp to commit other pages to memory and to brace myself for the next recitation. But at that the class was slowly creeping up on me. It was a sort of race between us. I had decided to outwind the bunch. We kept on doggedly for two weeks. Then the class began to lag— one of the boys had to drop out to help husk corn; the others, young women past school age, began to be irregular in attendance. I insisted that if we were to make any headway, these first principles would have to be mastered. Before long one of the girls got married clandestinely and was out of the class. The other decided to give it up and put more time on grammar. That was the last of algebra for me for a full decade, and could as well have been the last for all time.

I taught a good school, at any rate the patrons all thought so. I was respected by everyone; as I now believe, because I lived in town and they in the country. They unconsciously assigned to me a fictitious superiority. There was disparity in our complexes and it was all in my favor. Since then I have discovered that characteristic in many places. It is the difference between Dry Fork and Pittsburgh, and quite a fictitious difference it is.

I had forty pupils in all. The older ones, several older than I, were courteous beyond my expectations. We were not so far from *Hoosier Schoolmaster* days; and my pedagogical habitat was enough like that in Southern Indiana, as pictured by Eggleston, for me to expect insurrectional conduct.

I had but one such adventure. One overgrown lad had to be punished and I felt that a decent trouncing might be a wholesome example for the whole school. Had I kept to the Kramer technique it might have been avoided.

It so happened that the boy had a big brother. The big brother decided to trounce the teacher. I was called out of Old Salem Church one night when revival services were in progress and brought, all unsuspecting, to a group of young fellows gathered under a tree in the churchyard. The big brother declared his purpose. He meant to lick me and gave me an opportunity to take off my coat. I told him he couldn't lick me, though I was pretty sure he could; and I added that I did not think it would be necessary to remove my coat. I dared him to begin and was afraid he might. He hesitated unexplainably and I was emboldened to put on a bit of horseplay. I knew the fighting lingo of lower Dry Fork and it went at face value (as mere horseplay) all up and down the creek. I declaimed it glibly, minus profane accompaniments, as I had rehearsed it many a time in my imaginary boyish heroics. I was a better talker than the bully and was gaining some ground, I could see. The big scamp kept stamping up and down and executing hostile gestures and I still anticipated a good drubbing at his hands. But I was really getting a little peeved myself now and glanced about for a usable club.

Then came rescue. An old neighbor of ours, a man named John Batt from farther down the creek, came out of the crowd and faced the bully. "Shut up, Bill," he said; and Bill shut. Then John Batt squared his muscular body and dared any man in the crowd or any two or any three to lay a finger on the schoolteacher. The party was over. I went back into the meetinghouse palpitating tremulously but not by reason of spiritual fervor.

The two rural revivals were annual events of the winter months in that community. Rock Branch Baptist church held forth first. After that Old Salem Methodist opened up. The order might be reversed another year. Whichever got in first would burn up the revival interest of the community, work over most of the material, and make hard sledding for the other.

I attended these meetings as often as I could. I had designs on the gospel ministry. I was taking my first lessons, gathering, a bit here and a bit there, as I have always done. I recall vividly Jimmy Turner's sermon at Rock Branch that winter, on the text, "Two are better than one." And I recall the anxious-seat process of conversion then in vogue. It was a study in rural psychology but nobody called it that. Locally it was "a wonderful outpouring of the Holy Ghost." I drew many of my observations from hushed conversations among my older pupils. But others I gathered firsthand. Some in the community who would seem to have been worse sinners than their brethren, but who were not, had to be worked over every year. They were the impressionables. I think it did them good; they thought it did, and it cost nothing—it might have kept them out of jail. Others, of the best-behaved folk, never could "get through" satisfactorily. It did not mesh in with what I had read about the prodigal's father waiting for the wayward son's return and running out to give him welcome. But, with all the crudeness of it, there were, I am sure, many sincere outreachings after God.

My long drill on foot, twice each week end, lay along the railroad right-of-way. I always started before daylight on Monday morning. I kept always to the middle of the track for better footing. To pass the time profitably I visioned assembled audiences and rehearsed improvised discourses as I walked. Try as I would not to let this become known, it got out somehow. And the section hands who inspected the track daily made common talk that my exhortations were so eloquent and fetching that all fence posts and telegraph poles were white on the side next the track.

I did not ask to be considered for a second term of school at either Pleasant Hill or upper Dry Fork. Both places seemed to me to be mileposts to be left behind. Yet, so far as I could see, I must continue teaching. But I would study the "four sciences" and get a first-grade certificate that would command better pay. Steel's *Sixteen Weeks* series were our standard texts. It was a fancy of mine, still entertained, that I could learn by myself anything I needed to know had I but time and opportunity.

But I would have to be making something. I could hire out to some farmer for fifty cents a day in summer and could go on teaching in winter. Only by that plan I would be a long time getting into the better schools. I made bold, however, to apply for the intermediate room at the Geff schools. One of the directors was the brother of my sister's husband. With that leverage I lined up another of the directors. The third I found busy with many concerns and could have but a word with him. But he gave assent, as I thought, to get rid of me for the moment. Thus assured of winter employment I wrote to a farmer

111

I knew in an adjoining county and hired myself to him for a term of three months at nineteen dollars a month.

Away I went on the forenoon train north and paid the fare out of two dollars I borrowed from a blacksmith friend of mine. My mother had prepared a lunch, for I would be waiting at a way station at noon with no dime to spare for food. I was venturing out from home. There were stirrings within me I did not understand. While waiting at an intersection, I strolled out on the track and sat long on the end of a tie. When I opened my lunch, there was a piece of luscious rhubarb pie such as only my mother could make and such as she knew I liked so well. It was a strange sort of eye opener to me. I sat there a full hour longer without eating a bite. My tear-filled eyes were fixed on the horizon of that flat bit of prairie land but I saw none of it. I saw instead the little summer kitchen at home and my mother feeling her way around, a weight in her heart, as I well knew, like a lump of lead. My homesickness continued until I fell asleep that night. It returned usually on Sunday afternoons all that summer, but youthful spirits do not yield for long to such depression. I rallied and gradually formed a boyish fondness for the farmer's daughter.

Chapter 11

Working and Waiting

Should I ever be disabled or become inactive so that I cannot work with mind or body, I will not have to wait for death to relieve me—I will be dead then. Nothing bores me like a dull time. So I welcomed the prospect of a summer's work and went at my new assignment with a will.

There would be three months of activity out of doors—work I had learned to do and enjoy. Then I would return to Geff. The natives would be surprised that I was to teach in town. I swelled up a little over the prospect. I would soon be a man, for would not I be twenty that very fall? And, too, the farmer's daughter was very nice to me. My personal needs were almost nothing, checked shirt and overalls, socks and brogans, and a fifteen-cent straw hat. I was sending money home regularly; and the twins were now helping with such odd jobs as they could get about the little town.

That summer I whistled and sang as I worked. It was under the glowing suns of that season that I improvised my "endless tune." It was a quick, snappy air; and I kept up with it. Hour after hour I warbled it—to the horses I drove, to the cows I milked, to the trees and the birds, my whole body keeping time. Many a feathered songster must have peered furtively from its leafy camouflage to discover what competitor had migrated to that sylvan glade.

Though not fully grown, I was muscular. Given time and tools, there was no task on that little farm I could not compass, and I went at each one—plowing, harrowing, planting, cultivating, harvesting hay, cutting grain, threshing—with zestful ardor. On the Fourth of July that year I followed the self-binder in oats harvest, shocking the grain, and caught the last sheaf before it touched the stubble. I could follow the plow all day and then, after supper, contest with neighbor boys at athletic stunts in the hard road until darkness fell. Up with the sun, or before, I brought the team from pasture, curried and harnessed them, milked the cows, ate a breakfast scant in variety but plentiful in supply, and was off to the field. There were no eight-hour days. Dawn to dusk was the rule and chores by lantern light if necessity required. I asked nothing of that farmer save that he outline the work to be done and then let me do it in my own way. I wanted no supervision and got none. He said I did the work better than he could do it himself.

One major task stands out. Farmers swap work a good deal. It so chanced that several of us must work together at the moving of a frame house across a twenty-acre meadow under a July sun. I drove to the county seat to bring out the professional house-mover, one Mr. Krahl, and his outfit. That took a full day and delay, occasioned by a broken coupling pole, made it a long day. We were back and ready for bed at ten that night, and on the job at daylight next day. Heavy steel jacks had to be sunk in the ground to lift the structure. A track of two by twelve unseasoned oaken boards twelve feet long had to be laid for the rollers that would carry the building. It had to be turned where it stood, edged out of the yard, taken across the garden and into the meadow. The power

114

used was a horsedrawn capstan with steel cable for a hitch. Progress was slow. The track timbers and heavy wood rollers had to be carried constantly from back to front. It would be hard to imagine labor more strenuous under conditions more trying, but we were a rowdy bunch of young bucks. All the boss had to do was to keep things lined up right. Ten of us did the work. I was smallest in stature of them all, but it was my pride to do a full share of the heaviest work. We wore scanty clothes and perspiration dripped from our healthy bodies constantly. My muscles seemed strong as leather and flexible as rubber that day.

We were half done at noon. We walked across the remaining distance to a dinner of boiled salt pork with navy beans, cabbage, and other vegetables in plenty. We fairly shoveled in the food. I have always been a hearty eater, but that day, I surmise, would rank as the climax of all my gustatory performances. Yet none of us ate too much. One is not apt to do that with such food and such work as we had to do.

After dinner we lounged in the shade for an hour. When we were ready to resume, our employer brought out his jug of whiskey, customary then and there, and a small glass. It went around to each one but at my turn, I refused the liquor. The man with the jug good-humoredly urged me to take it but I would not. Krahl had a sharp eye and on further insistence he broke out with "Leave him alone; he'll do more than any man on the job without any liquor." This came to the ears of my own regular boss and he remarked about it one day. That made me feel good; and the farmer's daughter had her smile over it, too.

I was obliged to go home to Wayne County for the teachers' institute, for I was to teach in town. That was after most farm duties were finished for the season. My employer proposed that I ride home on the back of a fine young colt I had broken to saddle. That would save me some money; it was fifty-four

115

miles to Geff, and I had traveled half the distance before it came to me just why I had been given the use of the horse. The daughter and I were playing at the sweetheart game in an innocent boy-and-girl fashion; he thought I might not return if I went back by rail. With the colt on my hands I would be obliged to do so. He had proposed that I put out a few acres of wheat on his farm that fall. His clever ruse went far to banish my first boyish infatuation. I would not be so trapped. At the moment I was minded to return, leave the colt, and go by rail. But I had no money.

On the way home, though I rode at a gallop most of the way, I had time to think. I was putting away childish things. It was a somber day to me. Riding alone through the dust, under an August sun, mine were indeed long, long thoughts.

I had my own life to live. I could not live it as another young man might. I had had laid upon me, through the fault of no one, the burdens of a man. I had known and accepted them from the age of thirteen but what it might mean at the spring of adult life had not occurred to me before. I had as my sacred charge a half-blind mother and twin brothers, now thirteen, who must be kept in school. No matter what the prize to be won, I could not evade that responsibility. To do so would bring me far deeper hurt than keeping to the path of duty as I then saw it. All that day I seemed to feel a Presence hovering over me. It was a day like that experienced on Dry Fork at twelve. At noon, when I had fed my colt and had eaten my scant lunch, I stretched my body on a grassy place in the shade and read every word on the scrap of newspaper in which my food had been wrapped. I remember now, vividly, some of the items read and the new words discovered. When I arose to go again, I had something of the feeling that must have prompted one in ancient times to say, "Surely God is in this place and I knew it not."

116

That day I registered a vow that has been kept to this present moment. I would make the most of my life. I would educate myself in spite of all handicaps and hindrances. The world was mine to possess if I would. In spite of my sober mood and the long, hard ride through heat and dust, it was to me a day of illumination. I had said to myself, in substance, "I will go on preparing; my chance will come and I must be ready."

That night I was near enough to Geff to stop with a farmer acquaintance who gladly fed and bedded a tired and troubled boy-man.

Whoever has ridden fifty miles in one day on a two-year-old colt will not need to be told why it was that through five or six meals I stood up to eat. On the return trip I padded the saddle with an old cotton comforter and fared better. But I do not recall one single incident of the return trip.

I attended the institute but all to no purpose. For here one of those singular reverses that affect the whole future happened to me.

I thought I had that schoolteaching engagement cinched for good and sure; all three directors had promised. But when it came to making formal contract, one of them, the most influential of the three, had forgotten all about his promise to me and pledged his word to Dick Black. This director was decidedly embarrassed; the other two were provoked and would stand pat. But Dick Black, on the promise he had received, had put in the summer at school and would return confident of employment; and Dick was a friend of mine.

I proposed an adjustment that met the approval of all but brought distress to my mother. I would retire from the scene and release the directors from their pledge if they would let me have the principalship for the coming summer term. It was agreed; the salary would be sixty dollars a month instead of thirty. The contract I wrote was duly signed and I set out in quest of some sort of subsistence contact for the winter. I decided to take my borrowed horse back to his pasture and go on to Terre Haute where I might find employment. It disturbed my mother that her son, scarcely a man, would be away from home, a stranger in a strange city all winter.

I went to Terre Haute by way of the farm, just to return the borrowed colt. Pausing there I was induced to put in a crop of wheat I would never harvest. That now seems to have been part of a subtle plan hatched by the farmer and his wife. The farmer, now growing infirm, promised to help me buy a tract of land nearby and give me a start in life. Both he and his wife were eager for me to marry their daughter.

On the first autumn day that had the tang of frost in the air the girl drove me six miles to the railway station in the farm wagon. She confided to me on the way that her father had said that if I went away, she would never see me again. I resented the implication with honest emphasis. On the depot platform we kissed each other good-by and she gave me a flaming silk handkerchief such as the gallants of that day proudly carried. Her father was right. I never saw her again.

I was not happy the day I left. I did not know what was ahead and dared not guess. I had less than five dollars and would be on expense from the hour I got off the train. I was tired and fell asleep and while I slept, the train reached Terre Haute.

I secured lodging in a third-rate boarding house known as the "Ninth Street Hotel." I was to pay three dollars and a half a week for room and meals. I must have work within that week or else. I arrived on Friday; on Saturday I found employment with H. Alfrey Barrel Heading Factory to begin on Monday.

I went to Sunday school the first Sunday. The next day, someone stole my Sunday trousers and my silk handkerchief, carelessly left in a closet at the boarding house, so I did not go to Sunday school again. But something in the atmosphere had chilled me anyway, so that, trousers or no trousers, I might not have gone again. The people were very nice, I thought. One young fellow shook hands with me. The teacher of the class asked questions and when I answered with intelligence gained in the little church at Geff, looked at me in surprise, as did members of the class. But something was needed, and still is, to bridge the gap between rural and city church life.

My boarding place was not quite to my taste, though it was the best I could afford and was not far behind the best I had known. There was enough to eat, mostly food bought at the grocery stores; and the beds were tolerable. The boarders included an engine washer, a hunchbacked foundry worker, a grizzled old bricklayer, and a saw-mill man from over the line in Illinois. I surveyed my new associates with discerning eye. The engine washer was a windy chap who swaggered round the lobby disturbing everyone with needless talk. The hunchback was silent as the Sphinx except when spoken to. The bricklayer was a miser, always gloating over the money he happened to have. The saw-mill man, four years older than I, seemed to enjoy talking with me as he smoked his pipe.

I did not like to look at the hunchback; it scared me to get near him. I had a bed to myself, but the woman in charge told me that she was short of room and would have to send one of the other guests to sleep with me occasionally. When I awoke one morning, in the middle of the first week, I found I had a bedmate and it was the hunchback! We got acquainted as we drew on our trousers. His name was George Melton. He was a fine fellow, diffident but gentle and sincere. We were friends for the duration.

My wage was $1.25 a day, paid every two weeks. That was more than I had ever earned before. But when board money had been taken out and five dollars sent home each payday,

119

I had only enough left for laundry and haircuts with a dime each week for a detective story.

My only other extravagance was a nickel's worth of white taffy candy each Saturday evening, bought from an old man who sold hot tamales at a curb on Wabash Avenue. George Melton went to a show each week; I could not afford 25 cents for a seat in the balcony, and besides I had never seen a show and had not acquired the habit. George would describe the shows to me and warm up as he pictured the thrilling scenes. Poor desolate chap, shut away from others by his handicap, he fled from the hard realities of his lonely life to bask for a brief space in the realm of imagination that is open alike to all. While he sat through the show, I chewed my taffy and stared at things on display in the shop windows.

Present in my mind at all times was the proud consciousness that I was to be principal of the Geff school next summer. No stigma of the secondhand clothes and shoes I had had to buy for my work and no stultifying sense of humiliation because of the low level of my surroundings could dim that proud assurance. However, I must be preparing, so I sought out the city library. To take out books I must be a property owner or make a cash deposit. I was timid and did not know what to do. I could get glimpses of the long shelves of books but for my own reading I had to be content with reference works and bound volumes of periodicals to be had in the public reading room. I made good use of these, especially of one, *Littell's Living Age,* from which I gleaned many an unrelated item worth remembering.

My job at the factory was a problem job to me. I did not like my work. I stalked the shops and stores at odd times and applied everywhere, hoping to secure a different job at better pay. These were desolate days. They come back to me in memory whenever I hear the strains of a song that was new then; up and down the streets, everywhere, I heard it whistled and sung that winter:

> She's my sweetheart, I'm her beau,
> She's my Annie, I'm her Joe;
> Soon we'll marry, never to part,
> Little Annie Rooney, she's my sweetheart.

It was known by one or two at the factory that I had taught school. That gave me a kind of distinction, for my associates were an unlettered set. One day the tallykeeper for the piece-workers got hurt and I was asked to take his place. I did the work for one week until the regular man came back. I enjoyed the distinction even though it was not long continued, but more than the distinction I welcomed the prospect of an extra dollar and a half, for his job paid twenty-five cents a day more than I was receiving. I might pay that on a new over-coat. The only one I had ever owned was one bought second hand, and it had been laid aside long ago. But on payday my envelope was the same as before and try as I might, I could never get that well-earned dollar and a half. One might say that this was a small matter, but such disappointments have to be measured relatively; it was not a small matter to me when my weekly allowance for personal use was less than fifty cents. I had picked out a coat and used as guarantee deposit an old-fashioned hunting-case watch that I had got in a trade.

With a new overcoat I might have tried going to church and Sunday school again had not a triple misfortune befallen. I was laid up several days with a carbuncle on the back of my neck; then the engine at the factory blew out a cylinder head, which meant a week's shutdown. That brought us right up to the Christmas holidays when work would stop for a period. My always-scant surplus was soon gone, so I traded my watch to a man in the yard for enough money to pay out on my over-

121

coat and buy a ticket home. The storekeeper threw in a big gum raincoat, a revolver, and several other trinkets to equalize our estimates of value. I planned to leave in a day or two.

A railroad man I knew said to me, "Sam, you're not going to give the railroad any of that good money, are you?" I said, "Only enough to pay for my ticket." He chuckled and said he would show me a better way. He took me down to the station and explained how I could ride the "blind baggage" and not pay fare. I decided to do that, but the very next day a young chap of my age came in on the blind baggage and got killed in getting off. I was so shocked that I decided honesty might be the best policy after all, and so, like Jonah of old, paid my fare and went.

When I reached Altamount, where I was to change cars and might have to wait some hours, I had one lone ten-cent piece left. A kindly woman who had a little lunch place was closing for the day and sold me half of a thin custard pie of her own making for my dime. I had neither soup nor nuts and no warm drink to accompany, but I thought that the best pie I had ever eaten up to that time. I had been without food for more than a day.

I arrived at Geff late that night. My mother had no notice my coming. But her sensitive ear recognized my step on the board walk and when I rapped on the door, she said, "Sam, is that you?" The twins were up in a jiffy. It was as though a wanderer had returned, not a prodigal though. I had been in a far country among unfeeling strangers and was home safe again. We had no money and there was little food in the house. But of what there was I ate hungrily and then slept in the little bedroom as of old. My winter exile was over.

Back at old haunts with my chum again, we had much to talk over. He alone, of all the notables in Geff, knew of my secret contract for the principalship of the Geff schools. We gloated over the prospect of a local sensation when it would be made public, he no less than I; he was a loyal chum.

Then came word that there would be a vacancy in the old established dry-goods firm of E. Bonham and Co., in the county seat. I might have a chance there. I walked five miles on the B. & O. track to make application. Aristocratic old Ed Bonham had been in business there for nearly fifty years. He was a Methodist and he knew Mrs. Rapp. When I told him I had been in her employ three years, that closed the deal. I would be a salesman at eight dollars a week plus my room above the store where I stood guard over the bank next door. I was to do his chores, milk his cow, feed his pigs, mow his lawn, and fire the furnace for my board.

I said "Good-by" to schoolteaching. Somebody else could have that principalship. I had a better job—ten dollars a week, presently, and board at a table always bountifully spread. The food would be better, the chores less demanding, and social contacts on a higher level. And nobody knew or ever learned, even to this day, that I once turned down the principalship of the Geff schools.

PART III. Breaking Loose

Chapter 12

Over the Counter

Bonham's store carried a variety of goods—boots and shoes, women's cloaks and outer wraps, carpets and oilcloth, dress goods and trimmings, gloves and hose. There were no departments. Each salesman had to know all about everything. Our trade classified itself naturally enough. The bon-ton customer went to the head clerk and the saleslady. The middle-class buyers, mostly townspeople, were handled chiefly by the one or two employees next in rank to the head salesman and manager. Farm trade and factory customers fell to the cub, and, of course, I was the cub for about a year.

A gradual change was taking place all the time. Every year or two a new cub would come in and the incumbent of that lowly place would be advanced. No employee with a too-abundant self-esteem nor one who showed a disposition to avoid the less pleasant duties was ever advanced.

Selling may look very easy from outside the counter, but the salesman knows better. At first it seems impossible to master all details of the business from the faintest distinctions in shades of spool silk to the difference between two grades of sugar that look just alike. The cub is apt to feel the task as hopeless as did Mark Twain, when learning to be a pilot on the Mississippi. He must learn to wrap things decently—pepper that rolls around like leaden shot; "holland" which was then sold to line skirts and which is slicker than isinglass; linen tablecloths that, once unfolded, always refuse to go back as they were. He must learn to close the ends of his packages neatly and to tie them securely without holding the end of the twine in his teeth—all this in the presence of the customer who will be judging of his fitness for the job by his quick, dexterous movements, his neat packages and, most of all, by his gracious, gentlemanly bearing.

"Dimity, dimity—what's dimity?" That query flashed through my mind one day when I, the cub, had begun to discern differences in the fabrics we carried.

A woman had asked to see some dimity. "Why, yes," I said glibly, "we have some nice dimity here unless it has been closed out," and I fled to the head clerk at another counter and out of sight behind stacks of jeans and shirting. Instantly he relieved me. "It's white goods," he whispered, "you'll find it at the bottom of the first stack." And I did, with a flourish. "Oh, yes, here it is," and, lifting the loose end in my right hand where the light would strike it best, "Isn't that a pretty stripe?" It was and I made a sale.

The next year I had been promoted and another cub was on trial. One day he came to me, out of sight of his customer, and said, under his breath but in a towering height of exasperation, "Sam, what is dimity?" I told him and fled to where I might laugh unobserved. I have lived to learn that there is a lot of dimity in the world.

There were certain finicky and fastidious customers who would come when we got in new goods "just to look around," but who never bought anything outside of St. Louis. We learned these. We usually sent the cub to wait on them; I had my turn with one such bunch of young women and did my very best, others of the force looking on with amusement. I could not sell as much as a spool of thread. When the next cub came in, a tall lumbering chap from the hills of West Virginia, I had the pleasure of sending him to the front to wait on a group of daughters of one of the first families. The new man piled down the dry goods and dress materials abundantly, laughing and talking in loud, jocose manner that must have shocked his hypothetical customers. "Look at this, Jule," said one of the girls to another. "Jule!" cried our new salesman with a loud guffaw, "we had an ol' lame mule in West Virginia we called Jule." When they were gone, I told the new man that they never bought anything but always came in to look around. To my surprise he answered, "Oh, I knew that all the time; but I didn't care, I needed practice." He became a crack salesman. I never hear the name "Jule" that I do not chuckle. In one of my congregations a lady loved by everyone was affectionately called "Jule"; but I never could call her that because of that old lame mule in West Virginia.

At the beginning of my second year in the store I bought the Thorn house in which we lived at Geff for a home for my mother. I borrowed some of the money from a local building and loan company and paid week by week. We were better off at last.

I went home each week end, with but a few exceptions, the first year. As a rule I got away on the evening freight. That caused some complaint from others of the sales force who stayed on duty until nine o'clock Saturday nights. I walked back the five miles on the railroad track on Monday morning in time to sweep out the store before breakfast. In winter when weather was bad I might borrow a horse and buggy and be driven the distance by the twins. These were strenuous days.

126

But I had youth, plenty of good food, and an abounding ambition to do and be.

The two years I spent in the Bonham home had important educational value to me. Mr. Bonham's was the biggest and best house in town, for he was the banker as well as the merchant of the county seat. His son-in-law, who was county prosecutor and an attorney of parts, made his home there and we all ate together. At first I was shy but in time the embarrassment wore off and I was able to eat as much as I craved without undue timidity. The conversations about the table were usually on a wholesome level and instructive to such a one as I.

My sleeping quarters during this time were over the store which joined the bank. They had been so used for decades so that the occupant could act as a sort of guard for the place. My bedstead and bed clothing were old. Vermin had infested the room so long that they claimed right of possession. Periodically I made war with kerosene and soapsuds but could never exterminate them. There would be appeasements for the time; toleration; a "cease fire"; patience; and then a blitzkrieg with pause and interlude between clashes. Then the hosts of evil would rise again, numerous as Nazis and warlike as though led by some sort of pestilential dictator with voracious instincts.

The county-seat church interested me. My entree to religious groups came about through a preacher acquaintance. I had finished my sweeping after the five-mile walk from Geff one Monday morning, and was dusting out my broom at the curb when a man came leisurely along the other side of the street. He was a fine figure of a man full six feet tall, shapely, with a close-trimmed, auburn goatee, and the gait and bearing of a Chesterfield, elegantly clad in a tan Prince Albert with high top hat to match, a gold-headed cane in hand. I watched him go into the butcher-shop and then asked of a passing acquaintance who had paused for a moment, "Who in the world is that?" "It's the new Campbellite preacher," he said promptly. Then and there I decided to hear him preach. I heard once and thereafter stayed over the week end oftener to be in his services. His Sunday forenoon appearance before the little congregation he served was true to form. He was intellectually resourceful, emotionally well balanced, deliberate in his utterance, direct in his appeal to human nature, gifted with a rich speaking voice and a personality of rare charm. Two things kept him from becoming an outstanding pulpit man: an impossible wife and the lack of careful preparation for each public address. The one sapped his ambition; the other, in his middle years, thinned down his sermonic output.

The Christian Endeavor Movement came that way. I joined the local society and signed the pledge. I do not know that it made me better; but certainly it did me no harm; and the new contacts thus offered had educational value as well as a sort of polishing effect. I got a derby hat and learned to touch it when passing ladies of my acquaintance. This practice, brought into the Geff atmosphere, caused many a titter among our bumpkin bunch. I did not care; I am not sure but I was a little proud of it and kept right on tipping my hat.

The Sunday school crusade along interdenominational lines was being emphasized. Conventions—local, township, district, and state—were a feature of religious life. There was a demand for Sunday school speeches. I got into that in some way and was kept busy going here and there and getting experience along with publicity.

Then came a day, when I was not yet twenty-one, like that experienced at twelve on Dry Fork and that spent galloping home to attend teachers' institute on a memorable August day. Something began to stir within me. It was my practice, when the day's work was done, to read myself to sleep. For this I kept the Bible along with certain papers and magazines within reach.

One night when I opened at the Hebrew epistle, I came to this brief word, "This is not your rest." I read no further but fell to musing and drifted off into a deep sleep. With the morning, like a flash, came again that sentence, "This is not your rest." All day I could not get quite away from the subtle suggestion thrust uncannily into my mind.

I was not satisfied to sell dry goods after that. I began to collect books and renewed my reading. I subscribed to two religious journals and pursued them both with care each week.

When the farmer with whom I had spent the night on my long horseback ride asked me to come out some Sunday and make a "set Sunday school speech" at Dennis schoolhouse near him, I accepted. My chum and I harnessed his Morgan pony to a borrowed road cart and drove the twenty miles through May sunshine and road dust. We arrived and hitched our horse among the saplings as the closing song rang out:

> When He cometh, when He cometh
> To make up His jewels,
> All His jewels, precious jewels,
> His loved and His own.

I was introduced as a young preacher by my farmer friend. Youngsters wiggled and giggled, oldsters looked on with wonder. To my derby hat I had added a Prince Albert coat and pin-striped trousers. I must have been a figure to provoke speculation as I took my place boldly behind the teacher's desk.

I read a few verses from the New Testament and announced my text, "I must work the works of him that sent me, while it is day: the night cometh, when no man can work." (John 9:5.) I thought I had material for a forty-five minute address —anything short of that was only a talk. I had rehearsed several times with timepiece before me. *I got through in fifteen minutes.* We went home with the farmer for dinner and got away for the long ride home as soon as we could.

I waited a good while for my chum to comment. He seemed so reticent that my doubts were aroused. Despairing at last, I asked timidly what he thought of my sermon. Time passed, punctuated by the clop-clop of Morgan's hoofs while clouds of yellow dust enveloped our humble caravan.

"Honest to goodness, Sam," he said at last, "I never heard such a sermon in my life." I think he meant to tell the exact truth. I did not ask him to explain or make further comment.

Two summers were spent bushwhacking around mostly in schoolhouses, but a rural church or two made bold to open their doors to me. I usually had to pay a dollar for the livery rig I drove and the collection taken paid that back—but never much more than that. I was suspicious that the local college of cardinals thought a dollar was too much for what they got, and secretly "held out" on me.

My Methodist employer at the county seat began to hear of my preaching exploits. He actually took an interest in them. I did not know why until at the close of the second summer I chanced to overhear him tell a traveling salesman about it and add to his story this significant comment: "People from all over the northeast part of the county come in here and ask for Sam to wait on them." I think it could be established that preaching is an asset in the business world. What I did could hardly be called preaching as yet, but it brought customers to Bonham's store, and my employer was not wholly oblivious to the relation between business and religion.

I began to be known in the other direction, too; I was learning to sell goods. In the annual comparison of cloak sales I held first place in our store. I had come to be a factor in the establishment. Even the saleslady showed me a little deference at times. Ben McFarland, a traveling man, began to talk to me about a connection in St. Louis and gave me the benefit of his sage counsel every time he came round. He would say, "Sam, I can't imagine a promising man like you, who has won

130

the place you seem to hold in this establishment, giving it up for anything. In a little while you can be on the road with a trunk of samples and with a salary that would make your eyes bug out." More than once did this hard-headed man of the world thus exhort me.

Above all earthly desires that ever possessed me, I wished to go to college. I had been led to believe that a college training was the approved and only sure road into the gospel ministry—an illusion, as I now know. Some of our greatest preachers who themselves founded colleges were never matriculated in one. The Methodist minister at Geff, during this period, talked to me about being a preacher and mentioned the student's aid fund available to worthy young men who desired to enter the ministry. A local preacher of my own people, hearing of this, came to me to say that he would intercede with a preacher-training school he knew if I wished to go. He thought he could get some concessions in Walnut Grove College, perhaps secure a loan.

This would have been welcome information to me except that it did not fit my case at all. I was the sole support of my mother and my twin brothers, six years younger than I, must be kept in school. The alert young twins had taken over my old job of janitoring the schoolhouse in winter time and earned three dollars a month, fifteen dollars for the winter's work, which helped. Besides, our mother was not idle; all winter she knitted yarn socks for a farmer's family and took pay in sundry eatables. But our family stuck together. It would have been like treason to have broken away from that loyal group. I could not do it, I did not even consider it.

One Monday my preacher friend of the auburn beard came strolling by the store and paused for a word with me.

"Paul McCabe is in town," he said; "he preached for me yesterday morning. He has just graduated from Walnut Grove College."

I was interested at once; I wanted to meet Paul McCabe in the hope that he could give me some counsel. Next day the preacher brought him round. I was busy heading up a barrel of dried apples and had just driven the last nail. McCabe gave me a sweeping once-over and I, in overalls and astride the barrel, took hasty survey of McCabe. He wore a black Prince Albert coat and a derby hat and carried a cheap umbrella. I had marked his long, somewhat hesitant, stride and the queer manner in which he seemed to poke his way forward with the umbrella.

We talked for a few minutes in the presence of our mutual friend. McCabe told me it would be no use to go to Walnut Grove unless I had enough money to carry me through at least two years—three would be better though I might preach a little in the senior year to help out with graduating expenses. He was not sanguine at all and seemed to think that for me the ministry was a vain hope. It seemed that way to me, too, with the information he gave me. I was depressed over it for a day or two.

My depression passed, however, and I glided into a more courageous mood. I knew a young man could become a preacher of sorts among my people with very little schooling. I knew several who had done so. But I did not want to be that kind of preacher. I could be a successful schoolteacher, I knew; I could go on and up in the dry-goods business; there would be openings for such as I.

But I wanted above all else to be a preacher. My attitude gradually changed into something like that of a young farmer lad who desired to enter the ministry and decided to consult the Episcopal rector, whom he had once met. The clergyman heard him through, asked a good many questions, made some rather discouraging comments and finally advised him to stay with his farming. The young man was visibly agitated at this, somewhat provoked. He took his hat and slowly walked out.

At the gate he turned to his adviser, still standing in the door, and said, "You go jump in the lake, old mule collar—I'm going to be a preacher, I don't care what you say." And the story, related by the rector himself, declares that the young man became a distinguished pulpiteer.

I kept up my visits to rural schoolhouses and abandoned churches. I missed no opportunity to get on my feet in public if only to say a sentence or two. Those who followed me in these adventures were generous in their encouragements. Such as heard gave cordial attention and apparent endorsement to the bold, courageous noises I made.

I had read a book sometime before this entitled *The Theft of a Railroad Train*. It was a story of the Civil War. The tactics of the North seemed to require severance of a certain line of communication by which supplies were reaching the South. A train crew was organized for the expedition and sent, each man separately and alone, to a certain division point where the train men ate lunch. At the right moment the invading crew would leap, each man to his place, and leave the regulars at the lunch counter. It worked well. But the engineer, when he heard his train steaming out of the station, sensed instantly what was going on. He leaped from his stool, ran to the platform and started on foot, fast as he could go, up the track after his train. That would seem to have been about the most foolish thing he could do. But it turned out to be the wisest. Though the train left him far behind, he kept on running. At the edge of town he came upon a bunch of men with a handcar. He leaped aboard, the men with him, and away they went at a faster rate. At the next station a locomotive stood on the side-track all steamed up with its engineer at the throttle. The handcar was exchanged for this. The fleeing train paused long enough to tear out a rail, but, strangely enough, the pursuing engine passed over the gap, hit the rail on the other side and went on. It was the better locomotive of the two and in the end overtook the stolen train, dispersed the crew in charge, and frustrated the whole strange proceeding.

The instinctive action of that engineer intrigued me. There seemed to be a bit of philosophy involved. Not knowing what to do we must do the next thing. I have followed that rule many a time; often it has failed me; oftener it has proved to be the key to an otherwise impossible situation. During my last summer in the dry-goods store I applied that principle. I sold more goods, read more books and papers, made more amateurish speeches than ever before or since. In late summer a way of escape offered.

Through one of the religious journals I was reading regularly I learned of a new coal-mining town two hundred miles away where a little congregation was seeking a leader. They were looking for an unmarried man who could subsist on ten dollars a week. I thought I could do that since I had lived on less. I was not a preacher and it required an unwarranted degree of assurance on my part to write that first letter. But I had picked up sweet potatoes in a field for a share in the crop; I had dropped corn by hand at twenty-five cents a day; I had carried water to men working in a hay field; I had been chore boy to Mrs. Rapp for three years; I had directed and carried on the activities of a farm when its owner was absent; I had driven a huckster wagon over country roads and haggled with farm folk over the price of eggs and chickens; I had conducted all the business of a country store; I had taught school; I had spent a winter at factory work in Terre Haute. In every single instance the change from one to the other had at the first appalled me, but the transition had always been made successfully. I believed in myself. I was proficient in handing out *dry goods and notions*, I ought to be able to preach!

Once the letter was written I began to cast about tremblingly for any means I might use to strengthen my prospect of promotion from counter to chancel. I approached my friend of the auburn goatee. He responded instantly and wrote, voluntarily, to the correspondent of the church, a letter that dealt wholly in the "substance of things hoped for, the evidence of things not seen." I read that letter long afterward; its confident assurances would have sold a carload of ice to the devil!

I was asked to visit the little church in the coal-mining town. Clothed in my tailor-made blue broadcloth Prince Albert, to which had been added a new pair of pin-stripe trousers, and the whole crowned with a brand new derby, I swept into that pulpit and exploded one of thirteen things I had falsely called sermons. It was a bold, loud monotony while it lasted, but I felt that I got by fairly well. At the close the supply preacher for that day announced that he would leave the pulpit to me in the evening also. I had not expected that and was not prepared with another such "effort." But I got busy in the afternoon down among some willows by a stream and practiced up another speech.

That evening I met the board which consisted of five grizzled farmers. I learned to my consternation that they had thirty applications, fifteen of them graduates of Walnut Grove College, among them Paul McCabe. I presented my case with what grace I could muster and went back to the dry-goods store chagrined, crestfallen, crushed.

Ben McFarland, who came round soon after, labored despairingly with me. "You would soon be independent," he said. "You are on your way to a successful career in this business, and it is a good business. My wife and I are mighty well situated; I get twenty-four hundred a year; she handles half of it and we have five hundred dollars in the bank all the time— enough to meet any emergency. But think, Sam, what you have ahead as a preacher. Within a year you'll marry some girl in your church. In five years you'll have a wife and three children to support. On Monday you'll go down to the church treasurer for your week's pay; the treasurer will say 'We didn't get much in yesterday—only six dollars and eighty-seven cents; here it is, maybe they'll do better next week.' Then you'll go back home and say to your wife, 'We can't get the baby its new shoes this week and the grocery bill will have to wait.' Sam, that's what's ahead for you."

Ben was wrong. Some of this I have had to meet. In several instances it has fallen to me to put a stop to that abominable, slipshod, lazy way of handling church finance solely by freewill offerings. But in the main, the churches have been very kind to me.

To my great surprise and exultation I got the call to that little church. To the surprise of Mr. Bonham and the disgust of Ben McFarland I resigned as dry-goods salesman. My work at the store ended on a Thursday evening. I began as full-time preacher in a village pulpit, on the following Sunday forenoon. My congregation did not know this, of course, and I did not hasten to tell them. When a year had gone by and skies were fair, I revealed that part of the story to a jolly deacon. He blinked and grimaced and finally exclaimed, "That took some gall, I'd say . . .," and added, as consolation, "but our church sure gained a lot by it."

Chapter 13

Sojourn in Arcadia

This is a tribute to a place—the dearest expanse of good earth it has been my lot to look upon. There were never such prosperous farmsteads, such fruitful fields, such a sky as bent above, such a sun as bathed the landscape, such cloud shapes as went drifting by. And never were there such winter nights or sunny summer days among folk so gracious and appreciative. It seemed so because, of course, the season of glimpsing the glory of God in nature and in wholesome human nature comes to us but once.

No description of mine could cause the reader to see what I constantly beheld during the glowing seasons of my residence there. All ground was holy ground, every common shrub a burning bush, and the fleecy clouds in the blue depths above were as stately treasure ships to me, bound for some far-off enchanted shore.

With all this as a setting, each social occasion of more than ordinary significance and each event, planned or accidental, took on enlarged proportions and a warm glow of shining radiance. In comparison with what I have seen and known and passed through in subsequent years, all that transpired in a rural parish and among common folk ought to have faded into insignificance. But it has not; I see it all today as I saw it then.

Yet I do not go back there. I could not. I would not know where to go or how to find my way. If some friend of the un-opened eye took me there, I am sure I would not be able to see it again nor would he, of course. What my friend might see would be a drab rural landscape; what I would see might make me sick at heart. Yet through all the years I have been seeing it as I saw it then, and shall be, as I believe, forever and a day.

I see, going on there, framed and illuminated, amid such scenes the unassuming and untroubled life of a prosperous country community in Illinois during the early nineties. There are the people, the homes, the conveyances, the primitive roads, the schools, and the churches.

It is a moving picture, not in technicolor, merely, but in na-ture's actual garb; not on a flat surface but on a stage with figures not only life-size, but *alive*. They move about before me, passing and repassing, gliding in and out unhurried, greet-ing one another with friendly jest and the cordial badinage that is the best assurance of good will. They are engaged with the daily duties of commonplace lives, but, even when thus observed, they are to me great people. They were *my* people— my *first* people.

I see Deacon Sam again, ruddy, robust, rotund, plodding and puffing as he went about his farm activities in springtime; or on a winter night with a dishpan of tender snowy popcorn before him, the gaiety of early evening giving place to drowsi-ness as bedtime came near; or at church "with meek and un-affected grace," his face clean-shaven save for the well-combed, silvery mustache and chin beard.

One bleak night spent in the deacon's home has its throb in memory when I recall the family gathered round the great hard-coal base-burner until a late hour. My couch, a bountiful featherbed with wool blankets, was in the coldest part of a cold second story. The morning brought a surprising adventure. Before it was light, I heard the voice of my host in the yard below my window calling me. "Oh, Brother Lappin," he roared, "come down quick, the strawstack has fell over on my best cow an' I can't get her out by myself." I doubled and twisted into cold clothes, grabbed an overcoat en route and a pitchfork at the barn. Sure enough, the long-gnawed-at, toadstool-shaped stack had slipped off its icy stem and lay on one side on the ground. From somewhere within came the low moo-o-o of the imprisoned bossy. On top of the original stack was the corpulent deacon vainly prying away at the icy straw with a fork. As I came staggering over frozen knobs, his feet slipped and his body plunged downward between the stack and its overturned top. There he hung by his elbows, struggling mightily to climb out and regain his footing. From the ground there appeared to me a possible plan of deliverance. I thrust my fork into the recently fallen top and found it balanced and easily toppled over. But its removal played havoc with the excited and exasperated farmer. Down he went, lighting astride his cow. The imprisoned bovine matron came out of her grotto in double quick time, a look of injured pride on her countenance. She was as ashamed of it all as was my deacon friend, but far less confused and embarrassed. For me, I was convulsed with a merriment that still affects me when I recall the incident. My host had the appearance of one whose pride has been hurt. He said he could see nothing to laugh at. I did, and so did the family when I related it with all the frills at the breakfast table. However, pancakes and country sausage seemed to right things all round.

I see Mel Powell, bachelor friend five years older. On my first time round that twelve-mile charge, traveling on foot, I called on him at the farm he was tending and enjoyed the boiled dinner of kraut and pig knuckles he had prepared for himself. I tarried for an hour and went to the field with him. He loved me for that and I wondered that his respect and confidence had been so easily won. He was not a member of the church. I could not lead or lure him into the local fold. He traveled far to be present at my wedding, and brought me from afar to solemnize his own. I was then leaving Northern Illinois; he would go to the Far West soon after. Two messages from his wife came to me from his California home in later years—one to say that he had at last accepted Christ as his Savior and the other, much later, to tell how, while at work in the vineyard he loved so well, his life had gone quietly out.

I see the face of George Ball, that telltale twinkle in his eye, two dimples, and the half-mischievous smile, unmistakable tokens of generous good nature. He had been disgruntled to a degree when the old church was moved to town, farther from his farm by a mile or two. But his heart warmed to me when I spent a memorable week with him helping to build a hay shed. I had been in the home before and had occupied the commodious and well-furnished guest room; but on this occasion when he took me upstairs to bed, he said, "In there," pointing to the spare room, "is where the preacher sleeps; the hired hand goes in here," and he led to a smaller apartment on the other side of the hall, with furnishings comfortable but less costly. He doubled his subscription that year. It was his crack driving team that met me when I brought my girl wife to the new parsonage they had built for us. From his estate came the largest subscription toward building the new meetinghouse after I had gone.

"From his estate. . . ." It was June, and I was drowsing at home in the new parsonage. Corn plowing done, a group of our young married folk were away on picnic at a lakeside resort within driving distance. We would have been with them, if an unborn son had not claimed first consideration. At three o'clock a near neighbor rapped at my kitchen door and an

140

awed voice panted, "George Ball drowned at Senatchwine Lake." Leaving a neighbor with my wife, I hurried to a farmhouse two miles away where the Ladies' Aid was in session. The word I brought broke up the meeting, and I was off another three miles to Mel Powell's to call him from the field and, with him, make quick preparations for the long night drive, to meet the hearse.

I followed the fortunes of George Ball's young widow and four children through the decades and am an honor guest at their family reunion whenever I can attend.

Big, lumbering, good-natured Will Spangler and his plump, rosy-faced farmwife were attendants at my services, but not members of the church. I proposed to go out and help him with his corn husking. I arrived, with new husking gloves, as he was driving to the field. My husking had been from the shock; this was from the stalk. I had always said I could do what anyone else could do, but my practice did not measure up. "You take that inside row, Brother Lappin," he said to me, "and I'll take these two outside ones." I thought, "I'll show you a trick, Billy boy; wait till I get started." But as the horses moved slowly down the row, he began beating a tattoo on the throw boards with the hard golden ears and to keep it up, he had to husk half my row! I did not stay for the second load; I had to get my mail. But the noonday meal of sauerkraut and spareribs fitted me to face the chill north wind as I drilled back to town. I could not husk with Will Spangler; but within the month I received him and his wife into the church.

Vivid is the remembrance of revival seasons. They were protracted preaching meetings held every night at such season as would best accommodate the farming folk. That meant September or October, the "fall plowing season." That particular activity was a leisurely job. Summer was gone, crops were harvested and winter not imminent.

141

Emotionalism was not a factor, that peculiar type of mass evangelism known as the "union meeting" was as yet unknown. Our meetings had three distinct aims: first, to re-indoctrinate church members and iron out our congregational differences; second, to bombard the community with strong statements of Christian teaching; and third, to gather in any who might be ready to "repent and be baptized"—the phrase then used to indicate full surrender.

The evangelist was chosen and called months before. His arrival was an event in community life, an oasis of refreshment for the minister in charge. Fellowship was foremost. The minister and evangelist were invited to special dinners in homes, at the noon hour, and one or two pairs of the faithful from nearby were included as a rule. After a bounteous repast the women mingled the chatter of their talk with the clatter of the dishes as they "cleared away the things." Meanwhile the men jollied and joked or discussed church affairs as they pitched horseshoes in some convenient shade.

In the night services, neighbors would mingle to chat and shake hands before meeting time and join lustily in singing as the service passed its preliminary stage. But the sermon was central, terminating with an exhortation to rise and obey. Night by night, week by week, year by year, proceeding thus, remote groups from prairie and hillside and the larger assemblies in village and town gathered in "such as were being saved."

My penchant for fun has usually been an asset, sometimes an upset. Once at the Ladies' Aid Meeting, in an ancient farmhouse I learned wisdom and consideration by the humiliation and embarrassment I suffered. As I sat by the quilt where women were busy with needle and thread—and women's endless chatter—I saw a young mouse creep out of a crevice and venture along the top of the settee I was occupying. Young mice are not afraid, so I captured the little mite and held it in my hand, wondering what disposition to make of it. On the quilt was a thread box shaped like an elephant. Every now and then one would say, "Throw me the elephant." What did I do but gather in that box when it came near me and put my baby mouse inside; then I waited. Alice Beckwith soon asked for the elephant. When she opened it, out came the mouse on her hand. Never before had I seen a woman hysterical. A rattlesnake could not have frightened her more than did that harmless baby mouse. The incident nearly broke up the meeting.

Then there were the coal mines. The little cluster of two dozen houses with plain, retired farming folk, grew into a sizable city within half a year. I was sent to Chicago, all expenses paid, to arrange that every deed be so written that liquor could never be sold on the premises. But within the year, thirty saloons were in operation, the very ones who financed my trip giving consent. There I learned the secret power of the subtle adversary, the licensed liquor traffic. It is the cancer eating at the vitals of our boasted republic. The best thirteen years our country has ever had were those of constitutional prohibition, poorly enforced as it was. America will never be safe until the license infamy is abolished.

From nearby coal towns then, came streams of human drift, wastrel Negroes, unassimilated newcomers from Southern Europe who could speak no word of English, seekers after business, purveyors of vice in every form, lawless gangs with lawyers to prosecute and defend—mostly to defend. The quiet village to which I had come two years before had become a melting pot. It was too much for my little church. We were swamped by a thousand strange corruptions we had not known were in existence.

The new scene sickened my very soul. The charm of my rural parish vanished. The rural-trained church could not rise to the demand, the little preacher surveyed the situation and reluctantly surrendered and retreated sadly into another rural

143

field not far away. The experience had been a worth-while apprenticeship, however. I had not learned to preach. I never have. But I had got my bearings and made a beginning.

Time brought changes to the community I had left behind. In the new high school that came the sons and daughters of American farming folk were trained alongside equally intelligent youth of foreign parentage and different religious background. There were courtships and marriages. A new generation came along, then another and another, with the consequent blending of types, physical characteristics, and cultural heritage. I have lived to observe with reverent admiration how the great Father of us all, by laws and regulations established whole millenniums ago and destined to hold sway, in some degree forever, deals wisely and patiently with his great family.

I have gone back often in memory and I sense again, though dimly, what once I knew and felt of it all. Here were my first people, and my grossly irregular induction into the sacred calling. Here my initial triumph and my ultimate defeat. And here, in the midst of the once-familiar scenes I seem to stand again—and alone now. Thus, when I think back over it all. But lo, when I am there all is changed. The subtle charm of it has vanished, perhaps because I, too, have changed. But the church has stayed on. Staggered and confused at first, it presently arose to its task with renewed zeal and devotion. It has worked its difficult field well. I am glad I had a little part in the transformation of Old Antioch. I have enjoyed the same relationship, pastor to people, in other fields, several of them, but I have found no other like those in my Arcadia.

144

Chapter 14

Learning to Preach

No certified porter opened any door of the Christian ministry to me. I had to break in with presumption that bordered on sheer audacity. I now have, as I look back, something of the feeling of a thief or a robber who climbs up some irregular way. The scantiness of my preparation when I arrived in that Northern Illinois field to begin my first work appalls and chagrins me when I think of it. One fact saved me; my people knew less than I about what we were doing and therefore took a good deal for granted.

My work in that field was successful. It was said for years there, "Of course, we will never be able to get anyone like Brother Lappin." But it was not any merit of mine that wrought the fortunate result. It was, I am now convinced, the honest eagerness of a reasonably intelligent young man to make a success of his lifework, and the willingness of a patient, kindly people to be considerate and help him along.

There was this also. I was a living exponent of good will. Just as my teacher in the Geff school had won the admiration of his pupils and drawn out the best in his associate teachers by being a genial, sympathetic friend to them, just as he had induced his pupils to aspire and to learn and to do beyond what at first would have seemed possible, so I, mere neophite, almost an interloper, daring to thrust myself in where an angel would scarce have gone, must, first of all, exemplify and inspire good will in all.

That little church, guided by an instinctive intuition as to what was needed in their midst, chose me, in preference to Paul McCabe and fourteen other college graduates, not to mention a dozen applicants whose intellectual pedigree I did not ascertain. For the practical job to be done there, my experiences thus far provided a qualification more essential than could the schooling of those supposedly more fortunate than I. I doubt if any other of the several candidates would have done or could have done for that remote village community what I did. And I much doubt if any similar period of school training could have done for me what that church did in the two-year period of my service. The religious and educational process that went on was unconventional and unorthodox, but it was effective.

These reflections of mine come in later life, it will be understood, and after observations covering many men, many situations, and many years. In my earlier ministries I cherished a secret hope that I might somehow and sometime be able to get full college and university training. That ambition was the one living issue to me for a long time. I felt I could not hope to succeed without them.

Certain events transpiring around me added to my ever-present misgivings. Walnut Grove College turned out in that period some five or six bright and capable graduates who at once occupied the more desirable pulpits in the region. They succeeded and became active leaders of men. One, thought to be most unfortunate—a young man named Medbury—had had to leave school in his freshman year and locate in a small-town church. Still another, named Kindred, had gone out

146

under stress of circumstance and was beating about the bushes in a county to the southward. There were lamentations among faculty members over these promising young men whose ministry must be forever curtailed and handicapped, because they had not been able to complete the courses at Walnut Grove. My church was fourteen miles from the college. I knew the campus people. I heard the sage but somber pronouncements of senior students and professors concerning the inevitable eclipse that must come to these two men when youthful enthusiasm began to wane. All this, as may be imagined, would be calculated to stir misgivings on the part of the aspiring young preacher, as yet unschooled and doubtful of his own future prospects. If Medbury and Kindred[1] were doomed to obscurity by lack of diplomas and graduation honors, what of me, who had never seen inside an institution of higher learning!

Deacon Sam Skelton was my rural mentor in that period. He had had two years in Walnut Grove College along with men of his own age who had risen to positions of some note. He withheld no word of encouragement from me. He assured me that he was in a position to know what college training could do and could not do. He counseled me to go on and have no fears of success. But I had little consolation from his oft-repeated counsels. I credited him with sincerity but I did not trust his judgment. I knew that there would be but one time in life to get my college training and I knew that for me that time was passing by rapidly.

I lived in Mr. Skelton's home one year. He gave me the well-bound Greek Testament that had been left to him out of the library of a brother who had died at the threshold of a promising ministry. If ever I had an unhesitating champion, it was Sam Skelton. He believed in me and made me believe in myself. He even insisted that, given half a chance, I could

---

[1]Charles S. Medbury died at Des Moines, Ia., after a successful ministry in University Church covering thirty-five years; C. G. Kindred retired with honor after forty-eight years with Englewood Church in Chicago.

minister to the church in Walnut Grove more efficiently than the incumbent. But I kept both ears open, so that what went into one might go out through the other. I knew he was wrong—though he was half right. Very recently I heard another such deacon saying the same things about his young preacher, and I knew he was right—though he was half wrong.

When should a preacher student begin to preach? Should it be in his freshman year, his sophomore, his junior, or only in the senior? He should begin about two years before a dollar is spent for special schooling! The local church, the older minister, the disciplines and perplexities of life should be his first school. Given the equivalent of a high school education, he may make a measurably good preacher without further schooling. And in the two years he may prove himself to be one of the two in five on whom it is worth while to spend money for higher education. Out of such practice would come fewer misfits and disappointments.

During my first year a humane and capable evangelist conducted meetings in the church I served. He quickly discerned my great need and desire to succeed. With lavish generosity he poured out to me from his abundant store all I could absorb in the time we were together. Best of his service was the warm and unhesitating fellowship of an older preacher with one of his younger brethren. We went together into all the homes of that rural congregation, he as a man of years and experience, I as a beginner. But he kept me to the front constantly. At table, when asked to return thanks for the food, he often referred that distinction to me. If I spoke words of exhortation at the close of his discourse, as he might ask me to do, his gracious appreciations were always sincere and significant. He did for me what the worthy revivalist always does, he left me stronger with my church than he had found me.

I had brought a lot of books with me when I took up the work. The baggage man, when he lifted one end of my trunk, asked facetiously, "What on earth have you got in there—a cookstove?" I nailed up a shelf in my upstairs room and proceeded, as fast as I could, to fill up empty spaces with new purchases. I read, not as I learned to do later on, but much as a sheep grazing in rough pasture land, nibbling here and there, guided by instinct. I did no "light reading." I knew I would have no time for that if I kept pace with the demands of the work in hand.

I read religious journals assiduously. I did not stop at essays and news. I read the advertisements. I bought the current books and tracts recommended. I absorbed the truths contained and thus enriched my discourse with fresh, current religious thought.

I preached boldly enough, and that pleased my listeners. I made more mistakes than my hearers discerned. I had special reason to be grateful to one young woman of my congregation, a student in Rush Medical College, at home on vacation. She did not often comment on my public work but when she did, it was with tact and discretion. Whenever she spoke commendingly, I knew enough to await the discriminating suggestions she was about to make.

One evening at the door, while others were chatting and shaking hands, she asked me if I had ever seen a little book called *How to Talk* by Powell. I had not, but I made a mental note to get it. Afterward I sought her out and asked why she had made that suggestion. She told me frankly. I had made certain common errors, small slips of speech. I had said, "have sang," instead of "have sung." I had used the phrase, "between you and I," instead of "between you and me." These things would not matter with nine out of ten, she said, but that tenth person was the one I must look out for—he was important. And she added, "You see, you're not always going to preach in churches like this one." I was grateful for that remark and have recalled it often.

149

It was many years later that the teacher of English in a Western university said to me after a chapel talk, "It is a pleasure to listen to a speaker who guards his prepositions and knows how to use 'shall' and 'will.'" I thanked him, of course, and thought much of his remark. No schoolteacher, no course in English, no classroom lecture did that for me. It was the friendly suggestion of a young woman in the first church I served. Any preacher is fortunate to have a discerning hearer who will risk the wrench that friendship feels to help him in his beginning years.

In those eager, palpitating, outreaching years I missed no opportunity to hear other speakers, no matter who, no matter what their themes. I wanted to learn how the thing was done. A man with something worth while to say could spoil it all by not being able to say it well. I listened intently to every speaker and always learned something. Often, as I listened, I caught myself thinking, "That was a good start," or "He told the story well," or "His illustration fell short," or "That was a fine climax." To avoid becoming merely a critical listener, I made it my practice to seek out the speaker, when I could, and to commend some one definite part of his discourse. I had known the type of preacher who never has a good word for any other. I hated that attitude. Jealousy of another is the preacher's unpardonable sin. I wished to avoid it, and I did. No speaker, and especially no young preacher, ever has a more sympathetic listener than am I.

I attended many religious conventions. I could hear good preaching there—presumably. I did hear a half dozen discourses the greater part of which I can recall vividly—sermons by real preachers who knew God and man and who delivered their messages with fervor and abandon. But many a time I heard instead a well-dressed young pulpiteer of the new school read a well-prepared and nicely polished essay. These interested me, too. I learned to see in them certain fingerboards pointing into the ways of learning I wished so much to traverse. There were at that time, and in my circuit, gifted men of my own age with whom I became acquainted and whom I afterward learned to appreciate as associates in service—Russell Thrapp, W. H. Cannon, John R. Golden, Stephen E. Fisher, Finis S. Idleman, F. E. Smith, and A. A. Wilson. These were all college men of recent vintage. I watched each one narrowly and discriminatingly, and learned much. They all, without exception, became useful and influential preachers.

I was discovering that learning to preach involved a good deal more than preaching. Not only must I know the gospel which I would preach, I must know also the people about me— those to whom I would preach and those on the border with whom I must constantly be in contact. But more, I must draw daily from the vast field of human knowledge stored up in books. I had missed much of that. While conducting a limited ministry amid rural scenes I must be preparing for a larger ministry should such open to me. I had been starved intellectually. I had had but a glimpse now and then of the fascinations that lay beyond my narrowed environment. When released from former inhibitions and given time for the adventure, I reached out daily and with avid appetite caught and appropriated every fact or fancy, every intimation or inspiration, every crumb of interesting or useful knowledge. Mine had been a dark dawn. I must make use of every daylight hour.

My parish was full eight miles across. I had no means of travel other than on foot. Many a delightsome mile did I cover, book in hand, resting my senses from time to time, observing field and cloud and sky, wild flowers and prairie grasses, inhaling the breath of the open country, noting bird songs from hedgerows on either side. And then I enjoyed the guest privileges in the rural homes of happy humble folk.

I followed each fascinating lead as far as time and available resources would allow. This influenced my public address no little. I did not quote much from what I had read. I had heard that done in a way that the speaker seemed to be saying to those present, "You see I have read books; I know things; I am educated." I did not think that good taste. I tried to digest fully and restate clearly the substance as far as my hearers might need and understand.

A singing teacher came my way. I helped him get up a class. I had done a little, very little, in the rudiments of vocal music— just a chance experience of a few nights in a country singing school. But this man impressed me as knowing more than do-sol-me-do. We had good times in that two weeks. One day, after hearing me preach, he said, as we sat waiting for lunch, "Mr. Lappin, I believe I can help you to get a better speaking voice, if you will allow me." We went to the reed organ in our sitting room and he gave me the proper range of my voice. Then he prescribed a daily exercise for me. Before a mirror he explained that when exercising I must be able to see the small palate to make sure the sound channels were open. Then he said, "The Adam's apple is a sort of musical instrument and must remain stationary when you are running up and down the scale, else the throat muscles will cramp and weariness will result." "And the abdomen—it must always be pressed downward and outward by the diaphragm."

I practiced the exercises he gave me for thirty years; I still do them often. In many a situation my voice has been my credential. It never wearies; it is, I can say, almost never out of commission. Regardless of the quality of my discourse, no one complains of my diction or articulation. One lady in my Pittsburgh congregation carried an electric aid to make up for defective hearing. Asked if it was not an embarrassment, she said, "Why, no, I would not be without it; when our preacher speaks too loudly, I am the only person in the audience who can tone him down!" It is vital that a preacher have some-

152

thing worth while to say and just as vital that he be able to say it well.

I owe a great debt to one "Uncle Dan Eiklebarner," a be-whiskered old saint with an ear trumpet who used to sit regularly in the amen corner. I noted the eager look on his face as he tried to hear me. I resolved to preach that look off his face, and did. But he still used that tin ear thing. I resolved to put that out of commission, too, and did. Then I decided that as long as I had a pulpit, I would make everybody in my audience hear and understand every word, and that, too, without shouting. And, thanks to Uncle Dan, I have kept that resolution.

Chautauqua reading courses were in vogue. In one community I joined the class then forming. We had four textbooks. They were good solid material, popular in style. While covering my parish with horse and buggy, I read my texts. One night a week we met for review and discussion. A telescopic survey of geology, literature, and certain epochs of history was thus afforded. I was inching along; I could feel myself grow day by day.

But night by night, when I awoke in early morning hours, I faced the prospect of a ministry rising briefly like a rocket, and then falling and fading into mediocrity or oblivion. But what could I do about it? There was the little home at Geff on which I was still paying month by month; and there was the family of three for whose support and welfare I was chiefly responsible. Besides this, I was now the father of two.

It was at this time that I had to face up to a disquieting and distressing situation. I had returned to Geff for a few days. The little town had nothing for my two brothers, now that they had completed the studies offered in the public schools. They had no employment and the atmosphere of the streets and loafing places was menacing the best in them. I must get the boys out of there; and if I did, our mother must be pro-

153

vided for somehow. I had my own little family coming on, but I knew what had to be done. I brought the three of them into my own home, increasing the family to seven. Then, after a winter in the better school, my brothers worked on farms. As can be well imagined, my whole income (of fifteen dollars a week) and more was absorbed month by month. Debts piled up. Any merchant will allow the minister to run an account. The fact that a preacher's credit is good has wrecked many of us.

I got under the added burden with resolution but with some fear. I had to borrow a sum so large that it troubled me— about as much as we now pay when we trade a used Ford for a used Plymouth. And if it had not been for my indebtedness, I would have gone to college at the end of that ministry. I was near the school and had proffer of places to preach on Sundays.

However, our family had held together; whatever the level of our lives, we took it share and share alike. I had my assignment. I would not break with a plain moral obligation.

Books fascinated me. Someone loaned me one by Ella Wheeler Wilcox—*Maurine and Other Poems*. It was in a style that was new to me. I absorbed it. In one home where two daughters of the family had attended Walnut Grove College I found a copy of Myers' *Ancient, Medieval, and Modern History*. I spent months reading it. I picked up D'Aubigné's *History of the Reformation* in five volumes. I read it all as I did Conybeare and Howson's *Life and Epistles of Paul*. In one home where I lodged while conducting revival services I found a choice assortment of "handy-volume classics." That was a new field to me. It reminded me of our after-school readings with Kramer at Geff.

I flavored and varied my more serious reading, presently, by going through *David Copperfield,* the Dickens masterpiece, and its less well-known twin, *Arthur Bonnicastle,* by J. G. Holland. I liked these writers and followed on through *Nicholas Nickelby,*

Domby and Son, Pickwick Papers, and *The Old Curiosity Shop* and Holland's *Gold Foil, Plain Talks on Familiar Subjects,* and *The Life of Abraham Lincoln.*

One cannot buy many books when supporting a family of seven on a salary of fifteen dollars a week, so most of my reading material I borrowed. And I returned every book I borrowed. If others had done as well by me, I would be far richer in library treasure than I am.

I managed to purchase sundry volumes at secondhand book stores. Many were of great value to me although the cost was always small. Often, with fifty cents to spare, I have eaten a ten-cent lunch and carried home a volume or two from some dealer's dusty shelf. Of course, as my income increased, I bought sets on the installment plan. All preachers do that foolish thing, I suppose. In that way, I got too much of Joseph Parker, of Henry Ward Beecher, of the *Biblical Illustrator,* of the *Pulpit Commentary,* of the *Classical Library.* One set so purchased never ceased to delight me, however: John Lord's *Beacon Lights of History.* I read it with pleasure and profit now. Stoddard's *Lectures* and the *Little Journeys of Elbert Hubbard* were purchases I had no reason to regret.

I always had a penchant for writing. I am most happily situated before my typing machine or seated at table, pencil in hand and a blank sheet before me. I well recall the day I borrowed the use of an old Crandall, sleeve-type, writing machine to copy my first contribution to a national religious journal. That was during the first year of my settled ministry. I was not ashamed of the article when it appeared in print, but I saw at a glance where it could have been made better. It was never difficult for me to put words together harmoniously. That came, I suspect, from the wide reading and fond admiration of many favorite authors.

Printing offices entice and beguile me. One of my first calls in any new field was at the local printing office. Until the radio came, the office of the local newspaper was my receiving station. More interesting and valuable information "clears" through the printing office than through any livery stable or barber shop or even any Ladies' Aid Society in the community— or used to, at least.

I had anticipated that I would have to conduct funerals and marry people. My friend of the auburn beard who sent me singing into the ministry had supplied me a marriage ceremony. I had committed it with care, had had a wedding or two, and then one day came a call to perform a ceremony some ten miles beyond the bounds of my pastorate. I welcomed the invitation and was on hand, by horse and buggy, with a little time to spare. When I went to speak with the bride and groom, I learned that I was to use a double-ring ceremony. I had never heard of a double-ring ceremony or any ring ceremony. But I nodded and smiled and stepped outside with the excuse that I must blanket my horse. I did some swift thinking. An old preacher had said once, in my hearing, "The vital thing in a marriage is to get the contracting parties to say in the presence of witnesses that they will have each other; what else you do is only the trimmings." I reflected that the two rings had to be on exhibition somehow and had to have part in the marriage vows. I kept up a bold front and when I came to the contractual part, instead of saying "Do you take this woman whose hand you hold," etc., I said "Thus understanding the institution, if you desire to proceed, you will exchange these rings as token of your intention."

They were married and, I suppose, "lived happily ever after." A woman guest, present from Chicago, congratulated me on my ceremony. She added, "It was unique. I think I have never heard a ceremony just like it." She did not know why she had not, but I did: that ceremony was made to order and on the spot—I was on the spot.

It was in these days that I formed a profitable friendship with Millard J. Wood. He had graduated from a standard college, had spent three years in a theological seminary, and had had two years of advanced work in the nearby best-known university. But he had no pulpit. He was raising a garden in summer and husking corn in season, with sundry odd jobs on the side to keep his family larder running. He was a fine fellow, cordial and humble, and we grew to be chummy in off hours. He had a good library, read and spoke three languages besides English, and knew nearly everything he did not need to know to be a successful preacher. I bought several books from his collection. I gained much of benefit from my conversations with him. Once I asked him why he went that last time to study at the university. He answered in a slow, dreamy, musing sort of way, "There was a lot of things I wanted to . . . find out . . . and . . . I . . . I thought they could tell me there. . . . I thought they could solve some problems for me."

"And did they?" I asked.

"N . . . n . . . no—they did not," he said with troubled countenance, "and . . . worse than that . . . they gave me a lot more; when I got through I had twice as many disturbing questions as I had when I went."

I studied Greek one day, just one day. I had gathered certain helps intending to do something in Greek if I could, but I was busy that winter ransacking and indexing Conybeare and Howsen and had not got to it. I happened to make a call on the local Congregational preacher who was a scholar of some pretensions. I got the book I wanted and lingered. He made bold to set me right on a certain point in a recent sermon of mine he had heard.

I did not argue the point then and there; I was not prepared to do that with such a scholar as he. But I went back to my study bent on mischief. I got out my Greek books including a Greek English dictionary, the Westcott and Hort *Greek New*

157

Testament with Lexicon and Harper's *Inductive Greek Method.*
For twelve hours I studied Greek. The next week I dropped
in on my fellow pastor to return his book and in course of our
conversation I remarked, "Doctor, I believe you are wrong on
that passage in John; did you ever look up the Greek in that
connection?" He gave a start and said, "Why, n . . . no, I
never did." "Let's look it over," I said casually; he got up,
brought a stepladder and set it up by a tall case. In making
the climb he upset another case and as he gathered the scattered volumes, he said, "Oh, well, Lappin, it's no use for us to
argue over that point; we never could agree." But a few days
later I took over my nicely bound Westcott and Hort, and
showed him where he was wrong. He was convinced that I
knew Greek (which I did not); I was convinced that he had
forgotten all of his, as most preachers so soon do.

But I had learned enough about Greek that day so that, with
the help of Young's *Concordance* acquired secondhand, I could
use it as a tool, and I have done so ever since.

At the time of the John Alexander Dowie excitement, a man
by the name of Woolguth had come to our town of 5,000 population to do what his preceptor had proposed to do in Zion City
by the lake. Woolguth called in the lame, halt, and blind and
was holding meetings for prayer and healing in the homes of
church people. Several families who should have known better
opened their doors to him. The preachers became concerned
and talked it over. None knew what to do, so, presently, I vol-
unteered to handle the case.

I attended two of his seances and asked numerous questions.
Woolguth flinched and looked askance at me. He did not consider me a hopeful hearer, evidently. By dexterous prodding I
got him to say he was a Hebrew scholar. Next night I took
with me a Hebrew Old Testament borrowed from my Congregational friend. At a certain point I produced my book and
asked the great one to read the twelfth verse of the first chap-

158

ter of Genesis. He took the book, gingerly enough, for I thrust it into his hands, closed. Then he opened it as he would have done any other book and turned to the first printed page, mentally casting about, as I could see, for some way out of the trap. I relieved him. I said, "My friend, you are an impostor. You do not know Hebrew at all. You do not even know which side of the book to open. Hebrew reads from the back, not from the front like other books."

Then I stood up and addressed those present. "Friends," I said, "this man is a fakir like Dowie, whose stooge he is. He is deceiving you. Go back to your Bible and your churches and give up this foolishness."

Then to Woolguth I said, "And as for you, I would not be seen in this town in daylight after this if I were in your place. There is a northbound Illinois Central train at midnight—better get a ticket and take a ride." Of course, I was listed as a roughneck by his dupes, but Woolguth disappeared and most of his followers presently went shamefacedly back to their churches. Religion is not all sweetness and light. One must put up a fight for the faith occasionally. My observation is that when the fight is all out of a man, most of the manhood is gone.

I wanted at that period, above all else, to learn to preach. The importance of that work, the difficulty of the undertaking, and my own apparently ineradicable defects suggest the words of the Elder Broadus, "But I can't preach; I never have preached; I never knew anyone who could preach." But I am glad I kept on trying to learn.

Chapter 15

College Halls at Last

The village and country churches I served during some five or six years of my early ministry were all within a few miles of Walnut Grove College. Special occasions often drew me to the campus. I became acquainted with the faculty and many of the student body, especially the upper classmen. One might suppose I would have acquired a sense of ease and comfort in that atmosphere.

This was not so. Dark shadows of the past pursued me, the sloth and ignorance of Dry Fork, the sordidness and low idealism of Geff as it then was. Though as well dressed and as intelligent, naturally, I had not been privileged to pause, as had these, at the threshold of life and make needful preparation for service. I had but an eighth-grade schooling and a pronounced inferiority complex. My friends about the school were kind. They extended courtesies most generously. But many a time, when I craved to accept an invitation, I literally ran away under one pretext or another. I shrank in foolish dread from that contact.

When I matriculated at last, it was with a boding sense of diffidence and timidity that nearly paralyzed what slight self-confidence I had managed to build up. It was not what I found there, but what I feared I might find, that awed me.

These people were not my kind, thought I mistakenly; I could not measure up. In faraway Little Egypt I had heard much of this church school. My mental concept of Walnut Grove was that one might expect to find the citizens assembled in groups on the streets almost any time singing hymns and praying. Certainly there would be glittering domes, graceful spires, shining furniture, a literary atmosphere, ample walkways and always an air like that of Sunday afternoon in an ideal community.

This illusion quickly passed. I saw that Walnut Grove was but another county-seat town, its chief distinction a small college, poorly equipped and always struggling and hard-pressed for funds. But the spell of the college persisted. One scent of the laboratory, one glimpse of a class assembled before an august professor, one deep inhalation in that stuffy unventilated museum and I was off in a mental blue funk instantly. Somehow that atmosphere completely unmanned me. I was so ill at ease for a week or two that I could have wished I had not entered the school. But I had learned that one can overcome and live down such silly inhibitions, and that I soon succeeded in doing. I was to be one of the many eager seekers after knowledge—I, or so it seemed to me at least, the most eager of them all.

This had been my cherished goal for eight full years. I had not believed Paul McCabe when he said one must not expect to do any preaching until he had had at least three full years of college work. I had launched out with even my scant equipment and proved that he was wrong in this. I had found plenty to do, had turned from proffered pulpits to enter college, and now served one of the most attractive student supply churches.

161

Thus, much as I wished to secure this training, I had been made a little skeptical of its actual value. I had seen a good deal of the world and had formed some notions of my own as to what it takes to get ahead. When sedate faculty members solemnly lamented the blight that must inevitably fall on the ministry of men like Kindred and Medbury, I resented the inference. I knew these men personally and believed in them. And when class favorites came forth at commencement time, in a blaze of glory, wearing as a halo the blessing and benediction of their preceptors, veritable editions *de luxe,* I sometimes looked askance and dared to cherish a shade of secret skepticism. I had seen some such that had turned out to be duds in the battle of life. And on an occasion or two I had managed to get my little handcar on a side track alongside one of the big roaring moguls that was really doing well, and, by actual experiment, had discovered that I could hold my own. Mine was the harder pull and the rougher ride, to be sure, but I imagined that time, industry, and native good sense might go far toward removing even this handicap. The self-assurance of an Orson Welles or an Arthur Godfrey would have delivered me from this complex; but would not have helped me to become a good minister.

It will be perceived that I was not a desirable student. I had learned so many things by myself that I would not be content to sit still and be told things by another. Though far removed from childhood, I was precocious. Yet I was determined to have a full college training if it would give added assurance of success in my lifework.

In brief time my unhappy aloneness passed. I was enjoying a new fellowship. The thrill of it intrigued, fascinated, entranced me. There were books, books, books, good books, textbooks, books of history; the choicest of magazine literature; and with a faculty eager to give aid, as needed, to every questing mind wherever classified and of whatever calibre.

162

I was ten years late; I knew that—the more need that I lose no time. No one could be blamed for that already lost. When I should have been entering collage, I was earning a dollar and a quarter a day in a Terre Haute factory, sending all my earnings home to my family, my scant personal pleasure that of five cents' worth of white taffy once a week! So, again, the familiar imperative, "Run, Sammy, Run."

My twin brothers got to college before I did. A teacher of theirs in the Geff schools had a substantial measure of educational enthusiasm. Something akin to what Mr. Kramer gave me flowed from his manly life into theirs, and to Walnut Grove College they went, subsisting as best they could through two years of school life. That broke up the home nest. Mother could not live alone now. She would be with me or with her daughter when the twins were away. Looking back I can now imagine how she must have felt that after all her labor and sacrifice the whole foundation of her own interest and hope was giving way. We do not think of these things when we are young and ourselves ambitious to get on in the world.

During that two years, the twins began to preach. One of them would be sent to a nearly destitute and hopeless place to supply on Sunday while the regular student preacher went for the day where grass was longer. Whatever else they may have lacked, they had great measure of boldness backed up by the wide white shirt bosoms and Prince Albert coats then much in vogue and meant to suggest professional dignity. What a surprise it was then that the two of them, tired with the daily struggles to keep room rent paid and get the plainest of food, accepted regular pulpit work in churches able to offer a more substantial honorarium. Paul McCabe would have grimaced sourly at that, for they were barely in their freshman year.

Two years of this and they were back again the year of my matriculation and we three boys from Dry Fork were schoolmates and, in several studies, classmates. Two things we had

163

in common—an overmastering zeal to get through college and an overwhelming number of financial obligations. Having no money save the scant weekly income from student preaching worried us not a whit; we were young. The two of them meshed into the college setup better than I. My six years' seniority in age was at best a questionable advantage. I had to see college life through eyes long disciplined to observing the ways of the wide, wide world. No matter how long I stayed, I would always be a problem student. Always an irritating questioner, I could not at once subside and take everything as matter of course.

I was threatened with a run-in when my too frequent questionings aroused the ire of my biology teacher. But I stayed after class one day and we ironed it out. I told him to think of me, please, as one who had been before the world enough to know what I wanted; and that my questioning merely meant that I wished to get his ripened decision on certain evolutionary theories. He reacted happily and was my valued ally from that day on.

I had trouble in the Latin class. My teacher knew the subject thoroughly and believed with all her maidenly heart that the young preacher must know Latin and know it well. I could absorb it easily and did, but I suppose my utter dislike for having to spend my time reciting conjugations must have been evident to her. She never seemed to miss an opportunity to lay on the lash of sarcasm when she got me on my feet. I resented this, but what can a man do when his teacher is a lady?

I spent more time in framing diatribes against all mathematics above the multiplication tables than I did on any lesson assigned me. I reveled in my studies in English. I took note that practically every writer and thinker of distinction, save Sir Isaac Newton, Herbert Spencer, Darwin, and a few others, had rebelled against required mathematical studies. I was told that I needed mental drill. My answer was, "Yes, and I need physical exercise; I can get it turning somersaults or sawing wood; I saw wood—that gets somewhere."

All this amused my instructor in mathematics. One day when I had managed to give a satisfactory demonstration before the class of some twenty students he said,

"Now, Mr. Lappin, there is another way that problem can be solved."

"But," said I, "what's the use, if I have done it satisfactorily this way?"

"Well," he said, smiling broadly, "there are several ways one can go to the depot; it might be of some advantage to know them all."

And I could not refrain from responding, "But, Professor, if I wished to be directed to the depot in a hurry and an informant insisted on telling me all the different ways, I certainly would have to miss the train or go off and leave him talking." He laughed with the class. I was in a hurry then— and always.

I wonder that they could have had patience with me and my eccentricities. I still owe the friends made at Walnut Grove several payments on that account; I was so nearly incorrigible as to be almost impossible. One man in my classes who was near my age once said to me, "Lappin, I believe you would argue with a signboard." I appreciated that; more than once I have taken pains to have a signboard corrected, and once I took one down and reversed it; somebody had put it up "wrong end to" and top side down. There are a lot of the signboards of this world that much need to be argued with if we are to keep on right roads. It was by that technique that I found my way forward, the little way I have come.

I was ambitious as well as precocious. That must have made me even more a problem student. I did not know exactly what I wanted but I knew what I wanted to do with it and I was none too patient when matters that seemed to me wholly ir-

165

relevant were thrust upon me. I thought I knew more than the Latin teacher about everything but Latin; more than the English teacher about everything but English; more than the science teacher about everything but science. But just these things, that they knew and I did not know, were the things I had come to college to learn, could I have reasoned that way; but I was in a hurry and thought I could get along without them. I was being disillusioned.

My preceptors were considerate. I was given credit in full, and on my own word, for every hour I had spent in the schoolroom. In English I was granted advanced standing, privileged to take work ordinarily done only by seniors. One instructor said to me, "Mr. Lappin, you know enough to be a graduate of this school." I thanked him and expressed regret that the things I knew were not the right things. I now believe that what I already knew was of far more practical value to a preacher than the things prescribed in the course. Yet nothing can ever quite compensate for lack of contact with a college atmosphere. It was that that I needed, could it have been had at the right time in my life.

To meet financial obligations as nearly as possible, I had rented a house near the campus so that I could sublet rooms to students. During the winter I held two revival meetings, keeping up with my studies meantime. When spring came, I planted an acre of garden. We kept chickens besides. I had never yet known the limit of my physical endurance. I could work all day, study all night, preach twice on Sunday, and do chores as recreation. I lived that year, after my first embarrassments were over, on heights of zestful gratification I had never before scaled.

It was always a sore experience to me when at dark on Saturday evening I must walk the mile to a railroad station and take passage on a freight that landed me at my preaching point near midnight. I accepted it as one of the necessities, as did

166

my little family. I was getting a college education. No price we could pay was too great.

It was early spring when, one Satuday evening, we sat on the steps of our little porch waiting for the time when I would start to the depot. A great drowsiness fell upon me. I would have given anything to be allowed to sleep. It was with difficulty that I was aroused, but I got to my feet presently and made my way to the station and to a long seat in the caboose. The conductor had some trouble rousing me and getting me to the platform at my destination. Then agony followed and finally came the verdict, "Nervous exhaustion." I was sick but had no disease. I was in constant distress but never disabled. I knew all that was happening about me but walked as in a dream, seeing it all through a dim, hindering mental film. Half asleep all night, I was but half awake all day.

Doctors are good to have round us. They render invaluable service. But I learned this: when anything goes wrong in the cranium or the small intestine or the nervous system, the doctor is up against it right. There is a mystery of the secret places that the best of them cannot fathom. I had two good doctors to begin with. One assured me that I was suffering from nervous exhaustion and was in no serious danger; he made me give up drinking coffee, gave me some white tablets to take, and suggested outdoor exercise. I was already tending an acre of garden. The other physician found hyperacidity and gave me sour acid through a glass tube at mealtime with hypophosphites as a tonic. Neither had the least effect, though I gave their treatments, first the one and then the other, a long and meticulous trial.

I could read, think, and preach, after a fashion; but I could not keep up my schoolwork. I did not give up though; that would have been the ultimate tragedy to me. During summer vacation I traveled in the central states for the New York Juvenile Asylum, hoping the change would restore me by con-

167

vocation time. This proved a vain hope, however, and I had to leave school; I had no choice. Leaving school was a deep bitterness to me. No reverse of the many I have experienced ever cut me quite as deeply as did that.

I was never so completely defeated and done for as when it became clear to me that my adventure at Walnut Grove had failed and that I must face the world alone in my struggle to attain any distinction in one of the learned professions. And beyond all this lay the dread possibility that I was going into decline at so early an age and that I would not be able even to support my little family in comfort, nor further minister to my blind and dependent mother.

In my deepest distress I sought relief in special prayer, the most earnest prayer of my life. It was summer and the little town was nearly deserted. The barn, some rods back of the house we occupied, was as remote as any building of them all. The haymow of that barn was my Horeb of refuge that day. There in tears and agony I wrestled with my deep distress, God being witness to it all, as I truly believe. There I pledged all I was, all I could be, all I ever hoped to be, to a faithful ministry could I but be restored and set going again. I was, as I believed, on the very brink of total physical and mental collapse.

Relief was not immediate nor complete for many a trying day. But all I asked of God in my extremity that day was granted and much more, in his own good time. When doors of opportunity began to open later on, leading into other occupations far more lucrative, the haymow pledge held me, and I am not sorry. Once, later on, I expressed regret to a friend of mine, a dean in Illinois State University, that I had not been able to secure full academic training. His answer surprised me: "You would have been worth far less to the world than you are." When I questioned his statement, he added, "Sam, I know what I am talking about—you would be worth far less

168

than you are; I know what schools can do and what they cannot do; I know the human factors that make for success. You have had more than your share of them; go on with your work and be glad."

I landed presently in a corn-belt town of 1200, among good and considerate people, at a salary of fifteen dollars a week with parsonage, and in four years battled my way back to a reasonably healthy state.

The story of my gropings after a sense of poise and self-assurance may not be of interest to readers. But I dare not withhold such comment as may be helpful to another in like state who may chance to read this chapter.

One wise diagnostician remarked when he examined me, "You lack the nervous energy to digest food properly; the impairment of your digestion constantly limits your output of nervous energy; it is a hard matter to determine which is the vicious end of that thing." He called my ailment neurasthenia. He had named it, but he did nothing to give relief.

Osteopathy was nearly new then; I tried it with no appreciable benefit. Hydrotherapy was futile. Fletcherism helped some. Massage and suggestion did little good. Static electricity gave slight but temporary stimulus. One physician prescribed an exclusive milk diet, so I bought a cow; the next one declared milk was poison to me. One surgeon would remove turbinated bone from the nostrils; another would perform an operation on my eyes; the "father of orificial surgery" did his stuff; I read New Thought and thought little of it; I studied Christian Science but found no grain of wheat in all that chaff. Finally, I gave it up as a bad job.

Eight precious years of my life, already behind schedule, were gone. In this recuperative period I left off study save such as was necessary to keep my preaching up to par. I began to study birds and wild flowers, interests that would keep me in the open a good deal. Better still, I formed a boys' club

169

on the scouting level—Scouting came later, but I had two dozen pretty good scouts. I took the boys swimming. I gave them first lessons in bird study. Together we leased two town lots on which we planted potatoes and celery to buy baseball uniforms. We purchased certain athletic contrivances which we put up in a room of the church. We formed an orchestra and brought a director from the nearby county seat. I received all these boys into the church except those who were otherwise connected and all of these took membership in the churches of their parents. The community had lost a generation of young men. My work with boys stopped that leak, though very few adults appreciated it then.

These lads gave good account of themselves. Some years later when I went to fill a speaking engagement at Winona Lake Assembly my attention was called again and again to the fine musical combination, band and orchestra, then playing on the grounds. On special invitation I went with a friend to the pavilion where they were to play at sunset. We were there early and my first glance at the orchestra disclosed something familiar. I went among them and found nearly all of my club boys, now young men, with very few additional players. To me it was the thrill of the year. My imperative pause had not been fruitless.

To a Chautauqua lecturer, more than to any other man, do I feel indebted for final and full recovery. I had heard him through a course of health lectures. His talk sounded sensible to me and I sought him out in his tent on the grounds. He was eating lunch of the simplest foods. He did not touch me or ask any questions. He merely said, when he looked me over, "My friend, you are one of the multitude of us; you lived on the farm and ate everything in sight; you have changed your manner of life and have kept on with the old eating habits. You must learn how to eat or you will end up in the asylum or the graveyard."

170

He then instructed that I do without breakfast and drink water copiously through the forenoon for a period of three months; and that then I avoid animal foods for a considerable time and study to learn what foods and what combinations of food I could digest with best results. I did all that he suggested, and within six months was tough as a shoestring and have been for fifty years!

That was the day of local-option activity in the towns and villages of Illinois. I was in the thick of every campaign within reach. Impaired as I was, I found stimulus in the fight. Apparently we did some good, though places that went dry one year might swing back wet the next. Doubtless, our campaigning had its relative influence in the opening of blind eyes and the unstopping of deaf ears. But were that part of my ministry to be done over, I would leave leadership of that kind to others, to be called in by them as needed and desired. My reason for this opinion is that such campaigning is a side track and a preacher should keep to the main line. If the minister leads in a local crusade, he is a great fellow *when he wins;* he gets much credit among those favorable to the cause he champions. But if his cause is defeated, it is *his* defeat and in time his own people will unconsciously assume that their preacher is losing his influence. The fruit of gospel preaching, in all civic matters, is the Christian layman standing for the right in all his relations. It is the preacher's business to produce that type of citizen.

I am a prohibitionist. The best thirteen years America ever had was that period when our government outlawed the manufacture and sale of intoxicants. The most dastardly job of propaganda ever put over in a free country was that which, by grossly deceiving the public, brought about repeal. Prohibition or its equivalent will come again. There will be fluctuations back and forth, wet and dry; but in the end this government of ours will repudiate the system that would build up

171

business by breaking up homes, destroying lives, corrupting character, and promoting crime.

I have been astonished, often, at the ignorance of the body politic as to this matter of prohibition. Many are content to repeat, parrotlike, what they have heard from other wiseacres as ignorant of the facts. A professional man, supposed to be a well-read and intelligent man, once said to me, "I do not agree with you on the prohibition matter; you can't prohibit people from drinking." His remark was typical. It was never proposed to do that. Prohibition sought only to get the United States government out of the liquor business. Without the license system, that scourge would not be tolerated six months.

At the end of that ministry I might have gone back to college but I was thirty-four years old and I gave up the idea of further formal schooling. I saw clearly that mine was to be, through sheer necessity, another and widely different course. It had been my practice, up to that time, to learn things as well as I could and then retell them publicly, to others, in my own way. That had worked well; I found my knowledge of many matters constantly enlarging. I had always been able to say more and to say it better on paper than by word of mouth. In our earlier day-school examinations, even when I did not clearly understand something, I could convince the examiner that I had a grasp of the subject by the way I wrote about it. And by writing down the little I did know, I was usually stimulated to go on and learn more. It was thus that I was shunted off toward writing, a happy adjunct for the preacher.

PART IV. *Learning to Read and Write*

Chapter 16

Some Observations

The memory of my great need for some sort of typing machine during the earlier years of my ministry distresses me still. I would have used a typewriter every day. A secondhand machine could have been purchased at a low price, but even that was out of my reach. I borrowed one of primitive make a time or two. By merest chance I did get hold of one called the Odell, almost a toy, that had contended for place among the more elaborate and efficient machines. A preacher had discarded it, and I bought it for eight dollars. It did good work, but the process was slow and laborious. I wore it out and then bought a new one of the same make at the same price, probably the very last of the kind ever sold. I acquired sufficient skill in the use of these experimental contraptions to serve me well; but that mastery served no purpose when the better typing machines came. I had to begin anew.

On these two primitive instruments I wrote over a hundred columns of contributions to the *National Christian Inquirer* for which I received not so much as a slick nickel. But I was serving an apprenticeship in the art of writing and counted myself well paid. By that means I became, within ten years, as well known to the reading public of my own people as any other preacher in the state.

The typing distress ended when the *National Christian Inquirer,* in recognition of my contributions, sent me a brand new standard visible machine. I had paid for it, to be sure, and did so again and again, with voluntary contributions I was pleased to proffer week by week.

Three times in my life I have taken pride in material possessions: once when I owned my first clean, new lead pencil with eraser attached; again when a new pocketknife, with blades of good steel, was my own; last, and most notably, when I hauled that typewriter from the express office to the parsonage on a wheelbarrow. Not one of the dozen automobiles I have owned, nor all of them together, brought such exultation.

Haste had been sniffing and snapping at my heels ever since I preached that first rapid-fire discourse at Dennis School House. It pounced upon me and took me by the nape of the neck when I set that typing machine on the table. I should have studied the accompanying manual and learned to write correctly with three fingers on each hand. But I had an essay ready to copy and set about it with my two forefingers. I have done it that way ever since and I can produce as many pages of manuscript as can most who use six fingers.

I was a constant, if not always a discriminating, reader. For a long time I was limited to such books as I could get. I learned this, that not one tenth of the books printed are worth reading. The ones most worth while are the old ones. A shallow book, like a shallow brook, dries up early.

With periodical literature it is different. Newspapers, whether secular or religious, must present a varied and interesting issue on every publication day or the subscription list will melt away. These publications must keep alive and alert to be successful.

In the day of which I am writing a significant fashion was coming in. Dr. Frank Crane was publishing his "Pulpit Editorials" in a Chicago paper. George Ade was doing his inimitable "Stories of the Street and Town." Walt Mason was beginning his rhymes fashioned as prose. Charlie Bliss of the Montgomery, Illinois, *News* was issuing his whimsical and laughable monthly forecasts. These brief bits of condensed wisdom, wit, and humor delighted many. Readers turned to them with eager interest. Columnist writing was at dawn.

At that time I began my own series, "Fireside Philosophy," which ran monthly and sometimes oftener in the *National Christian Inquirer*. These one-column, chatty essays attracted attention. I found that they were being reproduced here and there, as far away as Great Britain. Men whose judgment I had reason to respect spoke kindly of them to me. One of these men, a college graduate and no mean judge of such matters, compared my style to that of James Lane Allen, whom I did not know then but whose books I at once proceeded to secure. This good friend was listed in *Who's Who* and proposed my name to that select fellowship. Regulation blanks were sent to me and the conditions of membership stated. I would have to tell the publisher about myself and then he would repeat to the uninitiated and wondering public what I had written. I then would buy, of course, though not required to do so, the fat volume for ten dollars or more. I own I was not deeply impressed. I have had my little smile all to myself now and then when some brother would turn proudly to the page in a ponderous directory of the self-certified elite and show me what the book said about him. Of course he had written it himself and had then bought a copy of the book. But that is the way they do it. That is the way I got into the *Religious Leaders of*

175

America and *Who's Who in the Middle West,* only it cost me twelve dollars! And that technique is the only justification for this book! I wrote it myself—about myself.

While I was thus ranging about, anxiously seeking ingress at whatever door, one opened to me unexpectedly. I inadvertently turned the key on a Monday when I was helping with the weekly wash. It was my habit to read whatever I had at hand between shifts as the laundry work went on. That day in the *Bloomington Pantagraph* my eye caught a facetious news item worked up by a Peoria reporter and printed first in the *Peoria Transcript* and then lifted bodily into the *Pantagraph.* It had other than news value to me then as had my whimsical response to it, and I am sure the gentle reader will allow me to reproduce it here as part of this story:

"WANTED, A CRANK PREACHER"

The trustees of Central Church, in Peoria, a large and influential congregation, met last night and decided that the pastor they should call to fill the existing vacancy in their pulpit must have the following qualifications: Not over thirty-five years old; must be married; must be an evangelist; must be a lodge man; must be a good mixer; must be a crank; must be willing to assume the burdens of his flock.

An hour after the clothes were through the rinse water, I mailed the following open letter to the *Pantagraph:*

Ashley J. Elliott,
Secretary, Board of Trustees
Central Church, Peoria, Ill.

Friend Elliott:

I have just read the little item describing the kind of preacher Central Church in Peoria is seeking. The list of qualifications desired is rather long, but now and then they may all be found in one man. For example, my own case:

1. I still lack a little of being thirty-five. True, I will pass that mark before long but I am not hurting with age as yet. I can set my foot flat on a wall ten inches higher than my head and can chin a limb ten times hand running.

2. I am married—and to a woman who, in my opinion, ranks well up with the best women I know; after twelve years of it, we are still living together; we have three children we would prefer to keep unless some church calling us wishes a preacher without children.

3. I am an evangelist; I served one year as state evangelist in Illinois and nearly killed myself at work. I got my own meetings and raised my own pay, but they let me be called "state evangelist." I have never, so far as I can recall now, turned anyone away who wanted to join the church if I thought they were in earnest about it.

4. I am a lodge man; I belong to the A.F. & A.M.; to the I.O.O.F.; the Knights of Pythias; and the Modern Woodmen. I would not object to joining others if the brethren will pay admission fees and keep up dues.

5. I do not know what you mean by "a good mixer." I am a little in doubt about that. I rather guess that I would do, though, for I have succeeded quite well on several occasions in getting things well mixed! Or, maybe you mean socially inclined. If so, I sure am your man. The person who comes near the church where I preach must be keen of scent and fleet

of foot if I don't shake his hand before he gets away. Sociable—well, I should say; why, many's the time I have crossed a muddy street to speak to a man—who owed me money!

6. I am a crank. Not a fool; but the kind of chap that moves things around. Things have got to move where I preach; several times I have preached such moving sermons that my family, household goods and all, got moved into another pastorate!

7. As to being willing to assume the burdens of the flock, I must be specific and cautious. I am not sure what you mean by that. I am willing to take charge of the pocketbooks of the brethren while they go fishing; I would hesitate to consider the big hats worn by the sisters at Easter time; I will not engage to salve the consciences of those who hurrah for Jesus and vote for the Devil; I will not usher any such up to the pearly gates; I will not deliver eulogies or write praiseful obituaries for church members who regard religion as a kind of insurance policy with brimstone clause, all paid up at baptism. About this last I am particular; if people will not come to church until they are brought by their mourning friends in a big black wagon, I am apt to be absent when they do come. If I can't preach *to* people while they live, I do not care to preach *about* them when they are dead, unless I am allowed to say what I please, and that is not good form.

Now brother Elliott, I write this letter just by way of encouragement; just to let you know that such a man as you are seeking may be found if you persist in your search. As to myself, I am preaching down here in a little town and don't wish to change. My folks are not like yours; they have never analyzed their own necessities as Central Church seems to have done. They couldn't say for the life of them what sort of preacher they need or want, but we seem to be getting along fairly well, and I would not move to Peoria or anywhere else for love or money just now.

The *Pantagraph* nabbed my letter much as a hungry bass takes a live grasshopper. The *Transcript* copied it with gusto. Other papers in Central Illinois followed suit. The Chicago papers saw human interest in it. Reporters from the lakeside came to interview me. The *Inter-Ocean* gave the story a whole page with pictures of my church building and of Central, in Peoria, of Mr. Elliott, and of me. Both congregations got lengthy write-ups. I had on file a hundred newspapers from Maine to Oregon that had published my open letter, some of them with editorial comment on churches and preachers.

My neighbor, Joe Nate, minister of the local Methodist Episcopal Church and a university man, came to talk with me about this interesting development. He told me how one William Allen White of Emporia, Kansas, had one day, not long before, penciled a hasty skit on "What's the Matter with Kansas?" and had suddenly found himself booted into prominence. He urged me to follow the lead I had. More than one newspaper left a door invitingly ajar, would I but leave off preaching and write.

I felt the pull of it all. Here, unexpectedly, the apple of opportunity had fallen at my feet. The thing I liked best to do I could now undertake. The decision I had to make was not easy. But my heart went back to my Walnut Grove vow, to Geff and the little church that had befriended the freckle-faced urchin who came gropingly in from Dry Fork. I resolved to go on preaching at whatever cost or sacrifice, and to write as a diversion.

179

However, I was not through with the affair, for a letter from Central Church in Peoria came to me asking me to address a banquet group. I accepted and then a call to that church followed. Without hesitation I declined with grace, for I did not like city atmosphere; I had a deep passion for rural life, for humble folk, and small towns. Within a year I accepted a call to a church in a village half the size of the one I was leaving, at a salary some hundreds of dollars less than that paid by the Peoria church.

My dislike for city life is native to me; it remains to this day. My passion for the little town and the little church was genuine; it, too, has endured. But I will not say that the choice I made then resulted from either. I wished to study. I might do so in the smaller field. Corn-belt conditions, especially the winter roads of that day, made pastoral calling impossible. In summer, farming folk would not wish to be bothered. I would have time at my disposal.

I did my "graduate work" in that little town. A good church building across from a comfortable parsonage provided a favorable setting. With very few exceptions I was in my study at the church each weekday forenoon from eight to twelve. I was able to make a survey of my previous gains, assay my acquirements, and discover my mistakes. I outlined courses of reading and kept to them doggedly. I explored the shores of human knowledge on my own. I pushed the prow of my canoe into many a fascinating inlet to survey the surprising attractions to be found there. I rowed out a little now and then to get a better view of it all and a sniff of breezes from the wider expanse. I hailed passing craft or exchanged salutes. Not many, I found, were as interested as I in exploration; most were bent on what the world calls "more serious business," meaning corn, hogs, and rich farm land, or recognition and promotion. Some expressed wonder at my quest for the strange, the beautiful, the hidden, and the unknown. Many wondered at my seeming indifference to the material and the matter-of-fact that filled the lives of those about me.

There were kind friends along the way who, taking note of my inclinations, thrust sundry books upon me, insisting that I read and report my findings. Sometimes this was embarrassing. I might not at the moment be interested in that particular subject. I always returned each book with some gracious word and usually allowed the owner to believe I had read it.

I took it upon myself to conduct a department in a weekly periodical published in Cincinnati—the donor of my typewriter. That required time, study, correct writing and punctuation, not to say hours of typing with my two index fingers. A preacher guest, noting my daily adherence to time schedule and the pains I took with my copy, wondered at it all and remarked that it seemed a thankless task if not a foolish one. I got my pay in satisfaction as I went along, and in money later on through a profitable connection of eleven years with the journal I thus served, preaching every Sunday meanwhile.

A physician, trained in the East, insisted that I read *The Riddle of the Universe,* by Ernst Haeckel. I managed to wade through it, gasping for breath at times in deep places. I thought that the great scientist could have done better by the common reader had he been a better writer. I was sure that had I been able to write as good a book I could have made it a much better one. But in our discussions of that book, the physician made it up to me by his casual hints on ordinary matters. He was old and had quit giving medicines; but his common sense about health and happiness did more good, I suspect, than much of his medicine had done during the years of his active practice.

Two suggestions of his have attended me to this day. He remarked once that the very best remedy for brain fag is interesting conversation, the exchange of ideas with another. I at once began experimenting and was astonished at the good results. I made many friends in that way. I was able to arouse the interest of others in things hitherto unthought of by them. I, too, had good returns in many matters related to life on humbler levels. But the direct stimulation of my own mind was my best reward.

His other suggestion was to the effect that to get most benefit from what one reads, hears, or otherwise learns, it must be retold at once and more than once; or, better, written down with care. Thus the borrowed fact or idea becomes one's very own intellectual possession. I followed that lead too.

I had as neighbor at this time another preacher of about my own age who was beginning to write, Harold Bell Wright. I read with interest his initial story, published first as a serial in a Chicago paper and afterward in book form. I studied its plot, its form, its embellishments closely and with a degree of appreciation if not admiration. One book after another came from the pen of my preacher friend. He grew rich on royalties. He left the pulpit but insisted that he was preaching still, only in another way.

The life of a professional writer is one of constant drudgery and distraction. Having produced one successful book he must at once go to work on another, and another, and still another, until his strength is spent and his life gone. I am thinking here of Harold Bell Wright, Peter Clark Macfarlane, Lloyd Douglas, and Vachel Lindsay. The distinction he may achieve is short-lived. His autographed volumes will soon be in secondhand bookstores. The money he may gain is poor reward for the pleasures he has missed—pleasures that money cannot buy.

I could have qualified as a writer but I could not have served faithfully as a preacher of the gospel if I had. I could create fictitious folk, put them in fit setting, make them talk in vernacular suited to time and place; I could imagine and invent situations, dramatic, romantic, amusing. But why should I take pains and expend labor in this way, when all about me were real people I could observe with interest, could serve, enjoy, and love? The main inducement offered was money and I could get as much of that as I needed while doing the kind of work that pleased me most. The distinction to be attained and the reward in possible royalties seemed to me but scant recompense for the sacrifice made and the labor invested.

I could write; I knew that. I tried it once as an interesting side line. I lightened my tasks for a season, sharpened my pencil, oiled up my typing machine, equipped it with new ribbon and platen roll and made a record of the romances, reverses, and roamings of the Huguenot family into which I happened to be born. I made six copies in duplicate with the sole intention of giving them to members of that family. It was a simple story told in six chapters. I was urged, by one who read it, to send it to *The Christian-Evangelist*. It appeared under the title, "Down in Old Missouri." The responses elicited, many of them on penciled postcards, surprised me. It fell into the hands of Hamlin Garland and William Hawley Smith, and both men wrote me warmly about it. A lawyer of literary tastes said: "I doubt if any writer since the days of Washington Irving has been better able to put on paper that something which, for lack of another name, we sometimes call magnetic power."

I had never seen any of these men. I did not wish to write as a lifework, but here I was being literally shoved into that field. At the insistence of a friend who was in the publishing business the six chapters were issued in a little book. It ran through ten printings.

Then I was invited to take up editorial work. I would not have to quit preaching; indeed, the work would be a valuable adjunct and, in turn, preaching would enhance my usefulness in the new work.

Seven busy, burdened years followed. A controversy arose among my people at about that time, over an issue that was of deep concern to me and that seemed a clear call to service in what was to me an uninviting field. The great mass of my writings for the defense of certain religious principles thought to be vital appeared in periodical publications.

My happiest hours have been those immediately following intense literary effort. My dullness, melancholy, pessimism are oftenest the result of congested, unuttered ideas. More, it is always the case that any happy expression of my best thoughts, either in public address or on paper, is a forceful stimulant to further and fruitful mental activity.

Good writing is simple, but simplicity is the most difficult skill to attain in any art. The simplest words that will pleasingly express the thought are the best words. The short sentence that states a single concept clearly is the best sentence. The briefest complete utterance of what the mind has conceived is the best literary form. The most lucid combination of rhythmic word and phrase is the finest style.

Good writing is truthful. It does not try to paint up things. It does not seek to display itself. The good writer unconsciously and unavoidably reveals himself. His product is himself written down. Pretty phrases, gaudy words, pompous style, studied alliteration, mar the page and betray self-consciousness. The writer, like the preacher, must be content to be just a voice.

To be truthful the writer must neither offend good taste nor court the favor of the fastidious. His words must be honest even though seemingly blunt or plain. A lot of good, wholesome, Anglo-Saxon words that are to be found in the Bible have been barred from our prudish speech. The Scriptures have a word for the woman who, for any price, barters away her womanhood; likewise for the man who lives on that level. If the Bible words were used always, such words would be needed less often.

Good writing uses no unnecessary words. I had to edit and proofread the work of one man from whose manuscript I could seldom check out a single word without doing violence to his thought. His was the best writing I had to deal with. There were others whose every essay or editorial benefited greatly by the omission of the opening paragraph. Poor writers they were, who inflicted meaningless or irrelevant sentences on the innocent reader while trying to crank up their mental machinery to the sparking point. Preaching, good and bad, is much like that; unless there be a striking thought clearly stated in the first sentence it is not worth while to keep tuned in. The radio has shown us how much can be crammed into a fifteen-minute period. No surplus words, no dead sentences, no mere padding there. Writing is hard work because it requires thinking, which is still harder.

The writer should know everything, else what he does not know may leave an evident lapse somewhere in his work. A slight error will often betray his human fallibility and send him tumbling from his pedestal.

The reporter who told how John Burroughs, when entertaining Edison and Ford, went out before breakfast, tapped a maple tree and drew sap to boil down for syrup to serve his guests at the morning meal, should have known better. It takes all day to draw a half bucket of sap and all day to boil it down. Then there would be but a spoonful of syrup. It requires fifty gallons of sap for a gallon of syrup.

The editor who tried to pay tribute to an eloquent preacher and represented him as taking a text from the "Second Book of Paul" should have known that while Paul wrote several "books" of the New Testament, none of them bears his name.

The Indiana author who tells, in one of her charming stories, how men came stealthily in the night to steal a "Golden Oak" tree from a timbered swamp ought to have known that there is no such oak, and no oak worth stealing.

Yes, writers should know everything, as should everyone. But if we knew everything, much of the pleasure of life—all of it, maybe—would be gone. There is endless enjoyment in forever gaining new things, new facts, new truth, new friends! Many young people are miserable because they have ceased to observe, to investigate, to learn. Many old people are always learning new things and are always happy. It may be—it must be, indeed, for those who are ever learning and ever coming to a clearer knowledge of the truth—that the richest and most enlightening lessons of life are reserved for the life beyond.

"Now are we the sons of God, and it doth not yet appear what we shall be: but we know that, when he shall appear, we shall be like him; for we shall see him as he is." (1 John 3:2.) That, indeed, will be the grandest adventure of all.

PART V. In Retrospect

Chapter 17

High Essentials

As I write, I seem to hear again three bells from my boy-hood—the dinner bell, the school bell, the church bell. Across the intervening fragrant fields of yesteryear they come to me with witching cadence. They seem to be calling me back to drink again from the living waters of my vanished youth.

Theirs is a voice from behind, and I cannot go that way. A commanding overtone bids me go on, and on, and ever on. But I shall go with lighter heart and firmer step for the memory of them. Let this be the beneficent ministry of all the precious past—to light the road ahead.

There was a day when I heard but one—the dinner bell. Then came that tremulous time when the school bell rang out its less alluring call. Then, in fullness of time, the church bell pealed. To me the sound of each one is insistent still. Their harmony is a perfect blend; my reactions are prompt and virile.

Some day I shall not be able to hear them all as now. One by one, I know, they will cease to ring for me. Some day this body of mine will neither need nor relish food. Some day this mind, always so eager to know and understand, will no longer function. Some day I will be able to hear but one of them—the church bell—last of the three to break in upon my consciousness with its imperative suggestion of an ever-vital need. It will be the last to speak its message of faith and hope and love. When that day comes, and I hear but the one, I shall know that the end of life's long trail is not far ahead; and I trust I may then be able to smile and whisper,

> There's a land beyond the river,
> That we call the sweet forever,
> And we only reach that shore by faith's decree;
> One by one we'll gain the portals,
> There to dwell with the immortals,
> When they ring the golden bells for you and me.
>
> —Dion De Marbelle

The horse that pulled my double-shovel plow on Wat Bestow's farm heard but one of these bells, I suppose; at least but one had meaning for him. Headed toward the barn we raced to the end of the row; plodding further afield we stopped short and there unhitched. Between the dinner bell and the school bell, or the church bell, is a chasm no horse could overleap and no clever theory ever span.

The dogs of the village heard them all with an agony of ear that found expression in loud and distracting chorus wholly lacking in melody. Dogs have always been that way, perhaps because, being dogs, they cannot go to school and church.

I knew a dog that would go to meet the children of the family, coming from school at a given time, and having welcomed them home would at once turn down another road to

188

meet his master who would come from the opposite direction fifteen minutes later. Never once did he go to meet his master first. The children took him to school one day and he was bored, quite evidently, with the whole proceeding. There were no classes for his grade.

One of the best-behaved and least troublesome members of my congregation in Central at Pittsburgh was a Seeing Eye dog named Night, owned by a blind parishioner. She knew us all and gave mute but kindly evidence of canine cordiality. But usually, when I had been preaching twenty minutes or thereabout, she would let out a dismal and distressed yowl of protest that diminished into a melancholy lament of resignation in which I could imagine the rest of the congregation joined with silent assent. The dog endured, though with protest, what others feigned to enjoy, because she had no notion of what was going on. That dog led her master to and from the university, many squares distant, until graduation day and stood beside him on leash in improvised cap and gown when honors were bestowed. Bored she must have been, and with no sense of the meaning of it all. But she understood and was prompt to respond at call of the dinner bell. Dogs (and some humans) are that way.

In the autumn an unmusical bell mounted on a framework over by the schoolhouse clanged out its loud metallic come-hither message to all of school age. I responded with a glad promptness not manifested by all. I had read Whittier's sweet poem, "In School Days," and wondered at one line—the one about feet that "creeping slow to school, went storming out to playing." The main attraction for me was inside. My hunger to know was deep and demanding. I learned at odd times, when serving as janitor, what was in every book in school. I spun the battered old globe round and round to get an understanding of what Monteith's *Advanced Geography,* with its flat maps purporting to present spherical bodies, did not make clear

189

to me. I turned the leaves of the big dictionary at recess time, looking at pictures and reading the titles underneath. I plied the teachers with questions almost beyond the point of endurance as I now imagine. Often I stayed after school, the desire to know transcending my appetite for food.

But eager to learn as I was, there was more than mere learning in that school. There were acquaintances, friendships, fellowships. And these, I was to discover out on the long trail of life, would endure when most that we had learned from books would be obsolete. They are still bright and clear to me. Faces of rustic urchins they are, of aspiring youth, of fresh young girlhood, unspoiled by the blights and deceits of a purblind and misguided world.

On Sundays the church bell rang out. I recall one Sunday morning at threshing time. I had had an arduous week on the Bestow farm, so my mother had let me sleep late. I had brought a book, *On the Jericho Road,* from the Bestow bookshelf and was absorbed in it as I sat on the shady side of our little house. The church bell rang. That played havoc with my emotions. I was so comfortable, I was inhaling deep satisfaction at every pore of my work-weary body. I wanted to stay where I was and, if anyone ever had good excuse to hide out from religious services, I had. I read on, page after page. Presently, before the last bell rang, my mother came timidly, gropingly, round the house and said, in a tone less of chiding than of sympathy and pleading, "Sam, aren't you going to Sunday school?" Of course I went; I am glad I did. That could well have been the most decisive turning point in my life, though there have been many, as seems to me now.

Once in my ministry I led in the building of a humble little chapel in an unchurched community. The question of a bell came up. One man, not himself religious, made a determined stand and gave his reason. "The bell's the best part of it," he said. "We won't all go to church but we'll all hear the bell, an' it'll make a difference. Some can't go but they c'n hear the bell, an' it'll remind 'em; some'll hide out and know they oughtn't to and the bell'll shock 'em; if there's to be no bell, half the people won't wash their faces nor blow their noses all day Sunday; yes sir, they'll be a bell; I'll raise the money for it." And he did.

One may have food enough and still be hungry; his mind may be surfeited with knowledge, information, scientific truth, the details and small talk of community life, and still be unsatisfied. There is a hunger that is not of body or mind. And to provide for that deeper hunger the church bell rings out its pleading, persuasive call to the souls of men.

What is done during the hour spent in a religious service may not matter much to those who go; it is the being there in response to a call of conscience that counts. The service may be a round of familiar ritual merely; or it may be the threadbare routine—two songs, reading and prayer, another song, and the sermon—or it may be but the inward searching of the Friends' meeting in olden times; it may be the silent meditation that attends the observance of the Lord's table after the ancient form. There may be music—good, indifferent or poor—a discourse, a period of social contact; that matters little if one goes there hungering for fellowship with Deity. Wherever he may go, the one who answers that call will hunger no more until an exacting world has wrought upon him again to steal away his spiritual power and vitality.

An overwise son questioned his mother, when she returned from a religious service, as to what gains she had for the trouble of getting ready and the time spent at the meetinghouse. She did not remember the preacher's text. She could not recall a sentence he had spoken. She was unable to say what hymns were sung. "Then what's the use of going, Mother, if you don't bring anything back with you?" Her immediate response was, "John, you take that basket and bring me some water from

191

the well." "Why, Mother," he said with surprise, "a basket can't hold water!" "That's right, me laddy," she said, "but you mind me an' go—it'll be a cleaner basket if water runs through it."

These three bells make a balanced harmony. They speak melodiously of the ideal life—life in three dimensions.

Whoever hears and heeds but only the first—the dinner bell— will become a carnal man. Those who hear and respond to two—the dinner bell and the school bell—will become natural men. But only those who hear all three, and give what response they can, will be spiritual men.

Developed in one dimension only—the physical—one may be compared to a pyramid, broad at the base but tapering toward nothingness all the way upward. Developed in the intellect chiefly, he will be as an inverted pyramid, broad enough at top, but with no physical basis. Those developed in these two alone appear as two pyramids so combined as to present a waspy center with broadness out of proportion above and below, a sort of hourglass figure. Only when the three vital elements in man are developed symmetrically and together do we see the perfected human being, alike in all dimensions.

In Ecclesiastes 12:13 we read, "Fear God, and keep his commandments." A modern man might reduce that formula to three words: earn, learn, yearn. It would not be far amiss to say that one's whole attention should be given to these three things from the beginning of youth to the end of physical efficiency.

It is a positive misfortune not to have to earn one's living; added benefits may accrue if one has to earn livings for others dependent upon him. Physical discipline, mental improvement, and spiritual growth are to be had in necessitous toil as nowhere else and in no other way. Our generation is loaded down with a surplus of golf players who have never learned to know the feel of a hoe handle. The tiled bathroom and the warm, silvery shower, with all the sweet-scented accompaniments, have contributed far less to human character than have the wash tub and soft soap used once a week. It is a serious defect in social life when so many eat what they have not earned while so many others constantly earn what they are not permitted to eat. In the long run, he who will not work ought not to be allowed to eat.

Next to a healthy stomach and an earned meal, the best blessing one can have is a passion to learn. The tragedy of most lives is that we cease to hunger for knowledge so soon. Whoever sets out to learn things has a lifetime job of increasing attractiveness and assured rewards in coinage of eternal worth.

It is not so much the kind or quantity of what is learned as the growth attained in the learning of it. Much we learn in school is soon of no further use; but, in any good school, the growth of soul that comes to us in the labor and process of learning will endure for the life that now is and also, as I believe, for that which is to come.

The nutshells, the outer husks, the dried-up pods of life quickly fall away. The body, once lithe, robust and athrill with warm impulses, will soon be but a piece of cold clay, the brain that governed it a handful of brown dust. But that is not all.

Man believes "he was not made to die." He believes there are bodies terrestrial and bodies celestial. He asks with Job, "If a man die, shall he live again?" (Job 14:14.) And by the faith he has in an affirmative answer, given at later date, he travels far and suffers much. It is not enough in the discipline of his soul for a man to earn his bread; not enough for him to learn the hard lessons of life; he must yearn—he will yearn and does yearn—for something above and beyond all this. And how, in a reasonable world, can one yearn for what does not exist? It is true, and he knows it, that

> The world has many a fond conceit,
> And our hope of heaven that was so sweet
> In simpler times, is now forlorn—
> The superstition of a creed outworn
> Which only babes and sucklings now repeat.

—Mary K. Bradley

But he knows also that these conceits and doubts are but the chill winds that blow at times off the bleak and barren wastes of human doubt and intellectual pride. They are transient, seasonal, and not for long. Like drouths and storms and floods, they come periodically but they are no part of the regular processes of nature. The warming sun of hope prevails through it all in spite of squalls and blizzards that disturb and excite for a time. And the soul settles back to its own confident intuition,

> For me, I learned beside a grassy bed,
> Where white arms of a cross are spread,
> And where heartsease purple with the budding Spring,
> That life, like love, is an immortal thing,
> And both shall rise, as Christ rose from the dead.

—Mary K. Bradley

That is life, sanely, properly, normally lived; its physical basis is a healthy body—it rests upon the earth. Its ultimate reach is heaven, and "the choir invisible, whose music is the gladness of the world." Its high purpose in the universe is to be a means of communication and transmission between two worlds. Its beneficent author and guardian over it all is the LORD Almighty, God of Abraham, Isaac and Jacob, our dwelling place in all generations. And underneath are the everlasting arms.

Food, clothes, and shelter are but the outer necessities of life, essential but not vital. Yet the grest masses of men spend the allotted span of years in accumulating these garnishments, and never really give attention to living. It is a tragedy that so many keep up this feverish race for tawdry prizes and the surplus that will never be needed and come presently, with shock of surprise, to where they must wade out, naked and alone, into the boundless, bottomless, shoreless sea of eternity.

So many writers have tried to tell us about life that in the multitude of counselors there is not only wisdom but also confusion. We learn by hearing and doing—we talk by hearing others and then mumbling stammered imitations, we walk by trying to do it and taking our falls as they come. Just as I learned to preach, what little I know about it, by listening to men who knew how and then trying it myself, to write by reading what others had written and then trying to put my own thoughts down on paper; so have I learned what I know of life from contact with life itself. That is a good way. The authors of books had themselves first to "wake up and live," to discover how to win friends and get along with people, and they learned mainly from hearing and doing.

When man was little more than a body, he would respond to the dinner bell and not much more. The oldest and most reliable record we have mentions a climax of creation when that body received an inbreathing of "the breath of life," by which man became a "living soul." Hitherto he could see, smell, taste, and hear—just the dinner bell. Then he could think and feel and resolve; the school bell was ringing for him. When this evolving creature appeared by virtue of an endowment more refined; the battle of the ages began. There was "a face upturned from the sod." The soul-man was having his day.

Ages passed—Job, in his misery of mind and body, pondered the mystery of human suffering; David, lamenting the loss of his baby boy, was confident that he would see him again; Isaiah, humbled by the consciousness of sin within himself and in the world about him, saw a far day when there would come One upon whom would be laid the iniquities of us all.

Then, marvelous final development, came the new day— the Lord's day. The church bell began to ring, bringing spiritual consciousness, faith and hope and love. "The first man is of the earth, earthy: the second man is the Lord from heaven. . . . As we have borne the image of the earthy, we shall also bear the image of the heavenly." (1 Corinthians 15:47, 49.) And we, children, grope our way out of a dark past, crying for the light until we all attain to mature spiritual manhood, "unto the measure of the stature of the fulness of Christ." (Ephesians 4:13.)

The man of flesh, who was of the earth, earthy, and the soul man, who bore some resemblance to spirit, had their day. Now, in Christ, he is a spiritual man—a new creature. Former things are passed away. Seeing all this, as did Paul, and as any thoughtful person must, what wonder that the Apostle, or any other, would be constrained to say, "Woe is unto me, if I preach not the gospel!" (1 Corinthians 9:16.)

"So runs my dream, but what am I?"[1] Just a preacher, that is all—all I have been, all I still am, all I ever wished to be.

---

[1]From *In Memoriam*, by Tennyson.

Chapter 18

Lowly Incidentals

The average human life is an endless succession of little things. One must learn somehow to manage them with grace and good humor or they will clutter up his inner self and keep him down in the dust and muck of godlessness. Being good is not so much in the daily effort just to be good as in attaining to the high degree where doing good will be instinctive.

Beatific moods and visions have a place, but for most of us life has to be lived among stumps and stones, crabgrass and cockle-burs, drouths and dust storms. To be sure, if we are to make an exhaustive study of the heavenly bodies we shall have need of higher mathematics, trigonometry, and calculus. But the great majority of our race will be able to get along on addition, subtraction, and multiplication; some have done decently with less.

We will be damned, if at all, by habitual, characteristic, unforgiven little sins. We will be saved, if through benefit of good deeds, by the unnoticed, unconscious little deeds such as spring spontaneously from humble, contrite hearts.

Not many great crimes have to be dealt with. Such as do take place are as a rule but the ultimate climax of some overgrown, insignificant trait too long let go uncurbed. Not many great, good deeds are required in the operation of such a world as this and those that do occur blossom out of the soil of wholesome, unseen human qualities. We would perish in the midst of our prideful prosperity were it not for the saving grace of the million habitual kindnesses of saintly souls, unassuming and unknown.

We abhor murder but indulge feelings of rancor and revenge that so easily lead to dastardly deeds. We would not steal, of course, but we look with covetous eyes on that which belongs by right to another. We shy away from terse, truthful words that relate to sex irregularity, but we tolerate without protest, patronize without pang of conscience, or even seek out pictures and reading matter subtly designed to inflame sordid passion and prompt lascivious imaginations.

There are high levels that are free from these miasmas that poison the soul. At these altitudes the saints and heroes of faith have lived, from Enoch, who walked with God in Syria's faraway shadowy land, to Abraham Lincoln and George Washington Minier whose lives were laid down on the prairie expanse of an American state. Here to do good becomes natural. The love of Christ and the Christian way have constrained until constraint is needed no more. The physical, so just and right in its place but so dangerously misleading when given free rein, has been sublimated. The heart has learned to prize and pursue the higher things and in that pursuit has found at last its release, its refuge, its joy.

The successful life is best attained if we make the best of three fundamental relationships—to self, to the world of people about us, and to the silent, infinite Presence many of us have learned to call God. Time and place are allowed for this in our allotted span of seventy years, but with none to spare.

First let us consider the measure of one's self—what he is, whence he came, what possibilities for good and evil there are

198

in him, and how far he has established control of himself. "What happens to us from without," says Harry Emerson Fosdick, "pulls our triggers and explodes us; the consequences will be measured by what there was in us to explode." For just that reason, to avoid sudden undesired and destructive explosions, one must know himself. Preparation for what one will certainly have to meet is a first obligation of every person. One will have to face his own world. Unless he faces it with cool, calm courage and dominates it he will be bested, beaten, and cast down by it. And here momentous issues hang. One may become, in his own mind, but a helpless creature of circumstance and succumb to adversity; or he may rise and look his calamities in the face and proceed, creatively, to overcome.

It is quiet we need, quiet and communion with the Infinite. Livingstone found it in the untracked solitudes of Africa; Paton among the dumb savages of the New Hebrides; Schweitzer at Lamborene on the equator; Kagawa amid the poverty, squalor, and disease of his own submerged countrymen. Episcopalians seek it through a perfected ritual; the Friends in their soundless assemblies; the first-century church in its self-examination at the communion table. Millions now find a measure of it through a brief period given to devotional reading and prayer at the beginning of each day.

Next to the need we all have, of confident composure in the face of a distracted and discordant world, is the will to do, to achieve, to win out. We are disposed to take the easy way. In the deeper matters of life that is never the right way. "If any man will come after me," said Jesus, "let him . . . take up his cross, and follow me." (Matthew 16:24.) There had been no such cross, when he said that. But many a condemned one had carried that hateful wooden thing out to the place of his execution. Jesus knew what the cross meant when he recommended it as a way to victory. By way of demonstration, later, he bore his own cross and died on it. Today his name is above every name, and the cross a universal symbol of complete consecration to the highest we know.

The fallacy of mechanistic determinism did not bother me. One thing I had learned to my entire satisfaction: I was not a mere machine operated by forces and influences playing upon me from without. I could recall a day on Dry Fork when a lad of twelve lifted up his sunburned, dust-begrimed visage among stubborn clods and sassafras sprouts and made a resolve. I had known a penniless youth who walked the side streets in Terre Haute to hide from the crowds on Wabash Avenue, the tears coursing bitterly down his face the while he swore and prayed in one breath that it should not always be so. And there was the young dry-goods salesman in his lonely room above the store to whom came the whisper, "This is not your rest."

Not once in these, or in a hundred other such stalemates, had I the benefit of one extraneous lift from some outside influence; not once had I waited for light to mark out the way ahead; not once had I asked for or expected help from those more fortunate. Rather I had often to refuse proffered counsel and choose my own course. Thrust forward always by some inner impulse and made confident by my faith in the ultimate right outcome of things, I had met and challenged impudent, hindering circumstance, slapped its ears down, faced it to a final knockout, and gone forward over its prostrate form.

That sort of thing produces a unique type of individual unlike the run-of-the-mine variety turned out by conventional processes. Whether it is a better type may be open to question, but at least it is different. My own opinion is that there could be too many such; they are hard to get along with. I have had difficulty getting along with myself, and that is one's first obligation.

We might at least be at peace with ourselves if it were not for the other selves all about who require to be tolerated, en-

200

dured, and placated. We must somehow be able to get along with them, too. How are we to get along with people of such varied and diverse training, such tastes, such habits, such ideals, such motives? If we could but keep to our own crowd, we might have some measure of peace; but we would be losers in the end; these life contacts are a discipline in themselves. The hermit does not grow. The recluse lives a pale and purposeless existence. Who flees life runs into oblivion.

How we get along with people and what we get from them will depend almost wholly on what we take to them. Unless our own eyes are "turned up from the clods" of this world, we get into many a wrangle and experience many a heartache. If self has been so subdued, so ennobled that we can go to them generously, patiently, considerately, we will make surprising discoveries and bring back heart treasure of enduring worth.

It is a recognized principle of psychology that one can elicit good will more certainly by asking a favor than by granting one. The reason is but thinly veiled. In asking a favor, one seems to say, "You are superior to me, therefore I am asking this favor." But in granting a favor, it is the reverse; one then seems to say, "I am superior to you, therefore I grant you this." Jesus asked a favor of the Samaritan woman and, again, of Zacchaeus, both difficult cases, and won both to his way of life.

Honest good will is at the bottom of all successful social and business dealing; it must be. It is an indispensable state of mind if any two are to agree on matters vital or important. Good will is a modern equivalent—or nearly so—of what the New Testament calls love, greatest of the abiding Christian graces. Another name for it is consideration. Love, as certified by the Apostle Paul, is not a warm, tender, sentimental thing. It is that rare disposition toward all mankind, the lovely and the unlovely alike, that would give every separate individual, no matter what his status, a square deal and full opportunity to make the best of himself. It results from the deep conviction that humanity is essentially one family and that each one of us, to the full extent of his opportunity, is his brother's keeper. "Peace among men of good will" is the sky-born assurance of a glorious new time when, to quote one of the great ones, "The wolf also shall dwell with the lamb, and the leopard shall lie down with the kid; and the calf and the young lion and the fatling together; and a little child shall lead them." (Isaiah 11:6.)

Peace can no more abide where good will is lacking—in a family, an enterprise, a world—than light and darkness can fill a room at the same time. That is why the first messengers of the Prince of Peace were not to stop long in a place unless the "son of peace be there." The son of peace is good will. That is why these intrepid advance scouts of the kingdom of God were called "the salt of the earth," the "light of the world," and their teaching the bread and water of life. They were the pioneer purveyors of good will in a warring world.

Church groups—where the ideals of Jesus are constantly exalted; where his mystical presence is persistently sought; where his followers learn to love even the unlovely—these are as oases in the moral desert lands of this arid, parching world. These have a life in themselves that will never perish from the earth. The gates of hell will not prevail against them. But every plant that the heavenly Father hath not planted shall be rooted up so that the seeds of the kingdom may grow and flourish.

Many problems tend to work themselves out if time be allowed. God takes time; and man is made in the image of God. He never hurries the hatching of a chick or the sprouting of an acorn by so much as a single day. It is ordained of God that the watched pot seems never to boil, for man is in a hurry and God is not; so many BTU's to so much water of such a temperature must stand for so long a time and no known artifice of man can hurry the process by so much as a single second. Our solar system is rushing on at incredible speed. Its destination is unrevealed and man can do nothing about it. The stars that looked down on Palestinian pastures when angels sang and on Canaan while the herdsmen of Abraham guarded their flocks look down on me when I walk at night among the sycamores of Leatherwood Creek. God takes time—so must we if we would have success in dealing with these human units made in his image.

One single passage in the New Testament covers all rules. It is Romans 13:9-10 where four commandments of the decalogue are mentioned and this enlightening word added:

"If there be any other commandment, it is briefly comprehended in this saying, namely, Thou shalt love thy neighbour as thyself.

"Love worketh no ill to his neighbour: therefore love is the fulfilling of the law."

Hence Paul could say in another place, "And above all these things put on love, which is the bond of perfectness." (Colossians 3:14.) Why did he say, "Above all these things put on love"? Because, properly put on, it made the whole list of limiting regulations unnecessary. Rules fail and pass; love never does.

There is, however, a crooked and perverse generation to be dealt with. Presently we are out of poise, spiritually. The clouds gather again and we find our feet sinking in the same old slough of despond. A jarring, discordant world has been too much for us. The radiance of that first joy is dimmed. What then? A day and place has been set for readjustment, the Lord's Day and the assembly of saints for self-examination at the table of the Lord. It is unfortunate for the church of today that all disciples do not, as a rule, meet on the first day of the week to break bread. That primitive practice ought to be restored. Christians ought to hear a sermon, to enjoy good

203

music, to meet congenial folk. But what of those driven souls who have no ear for sermon, who have no training for music, who are of no particular social group? Not all can have access to or can enjoy these garnishments of worship; but all can engage in self-examination and communion with the Lord on the Lord's Day. It is there the blessed restoration takes place. From there we may go out renewed and recharged with spiritual power to encounter life and its disciplines again. Better that by far than to have listened to music or heard a sermon or to have greeted certain of our social set.

In the African cattle country there is a terrible fly that drives poor brutes mad. They fight it off as best they can for a time but in vain; the pests persist and follow the herd in swarms. Then an instinct seizes the cattle and they stampede from the plains to the foothills and then to the mountain sides. The flies cannot live on the higher levels. That is the only escape —theirs and ours—the higher level.

It is the testimony of many and it is mine, too, that man cannot free himself from sin. Always when he would do good, evil is present with him. I think no number of rules would have helped me much; rules never did me much good. But I fled to a higher level, to the divine presence, the society of Christians, the church. That, let me here confess, was ever my refuge and my salvation.

> How firm a foundation, ye saints of the Lord,
> Is laid for your faith in His excellent word!
> What more can He say than to you He hath said,
> To you who for refuge to Jesus have fled.

Therein is hope, and it is our only hope. It is as an anchor cast into the mists of the future.

Chapter 19

The Women in It

Many good men have given credit to their mothers for the success attained and the esteem enjoyed among their fellows. Others who should have done so have ignored the debt they owe, and have claimed credit for themselves. That is an account that can never be squared until the judgment day. It was a knowing versifier who indited these lines:

> They talk about woman's sphere
> As though it had a limit.
>
> . . . .
>
> There's not a blessing or a woe;
> There's not a whispered "yes" or "no,"
> There's not a life, or death, or birth,
> That has a feather's weight of worth
> Without a woman in it.
>
> *—Kate Field*

My own mother, to whom I owe most, whose righteous wrath was so terribly aroused by the avarice of our tight-fisted neighbor, was the gentlest of women in all the natural feminine relationships of life. It was only when she must do a man's part in defense of her offspring that the instinct to condemn or hurt flamed forth.

It was when she was well past eighty that she stole into the room one day where I was busy at the typewriter, trying to frame a first sentence. I heard her slight movement and turned as she came gropingly toward me.

"Where are you, Samuel?" she called, and I caught one of her outstretched hands. It was seldom she called me "Samuel."

"I'm here at the table, Mother. What do you want?"

She came near and, with those sensitive fingers of hers, proceeded to look me over by means of that delicate, revealing touch that is nature's compensation when eyesight fails. Head, shoulders, arms, ears, and every feature of my face—she inspected them all with meticulous care in her tender painstaking way. There was no kiss, no embrace—the good Quaker folk of her day were reticent in speech and reserved in any expression of the deeper emotions. But I somehow sensed the impulse that had brought her to me and waited for some revealing word.

"What are you doing today?" she asked, presently.

"Writing a Sunday school lesson," I answered.

"What is it about?" came the inquiry, natural to her, for she had been reading the Bible in raised print for thirty years and knew the Scriptures well.

"It's about Hannah and Samuel this week," I said.

"Hannah and Samuel!" and mixed emotions of surprise, pleasure and seriousness swept her expressive face.

"Hannah and Samuel," she said again, "I always loved that story. My name is Hannah and I named you Samuel before you were born. I gave you to the Lord then. I brought up all of you on prayer; it was all I had to give you—all I could do for you, many a time."

206

I should have taken her in my arms, then, for a revealing talk. But I did not and the regret haunts me to this day. Men are so often that way in this busy unfeeling world.

The heart of a woman is deep and expansive. There is no standard by which to measure it. It contains much, I am sure, that only God can ever know. Only one of four Gospel writers, Luke, the young Greek physician, ventures into that unexplored realm, and he with only one sentence: "But Mary kept all these things and pondered them in her heart." (Luke 2:19.) Only Mary herself could have told Luke that and only Luke, the gentle young scholar, so appreciated its meaning as to preserve it in the deathless record.

Motherhood is a remarkable heritage. Even the maimed, the lame, the blind, the sinful, and unfavored rise to unimaginable levels through the experience of that function of a woman's life. I think now of one such out of many I have known. A spastic affliction had distorted her body and made speech difficult, but did not disturb her mental faculties. Her whole life must have been a martyrdom. Her husband, never her equal in intelligence, was invalided in an accident early in their married life. Their son was a sprightly, intelligent high school student, and with her counsel and care, was readying himself for usefulness in the days ahead. I was an invited guest in that humble home. The meal we ate together was, as I could well understand, a real work of art. That maimed mother had done eight washings for her neighbors that week to support those she loved and have me as her guest. To sit at that table, notwithstanding the drab atmosphere, was as a sacrament to me. I have never felt nearer to the Lord than in that hour. I was thinking then and thereafter, "Behold what God hath wrought through Christian motherhood!"

My own mother had worked enough and worried enough to kill ten women, if such things can kill. And when she fell asleep at ninety—her work done, her troubles ended, her faith triumphant—not one of the five of us could shed a tear, but every one had learned anew:

> The heart speaks most when the lips move not
> And the eye speaks a gentle goodbye.

My second mother, "Auntie Rapp," meticulous, austere, and ever alert to vital things, did for me what no other could have done. The trends toward youthful delinquency, as yet unnamed, would have been too much for my own busy and sadly handicapped mother. But Mrs. Rapp had brought her own son successfully through the treacherous moral morass of ignoble influences and was ready, with wisdom and experience thus learned, to guard my upbringing. That first night I slept in a room next to hers with only a board partition between. Before I slept, I heard her read the Bible and get down on her knees to pray. I could hear every word. When she had held up her own son, absent from home and among strangers, for such blessings as a merciful God might be pleased to bestow, she besought divine benefits for "the little boy Sammy, who has come to be with me here." Listening, I was impressed, awed, and comforted. I wondered if all mothers prayed for their sons when they were away—if mine did. The subtle influence of that hour has followed me to this day.

Once again her tender regard for me filtered through her puritanic reserve. With her consent I had attended a Fourth of July celebration at a rural meetinghouse four miles distant. I walked there and back. It was a great day for me. At the store that evening she asked, kindly, who I ate dinner with. I told her I had not had any dinner—I had been too shy and bashful to accept any of the several invitations extended. Her eyes filled with tears; she went at once to prepare food for me; and when she told Billy Blackburn, her Methodist confidant, about it, I was listening covertly out of sight and I heard her voice tremble with emotion.

When she was past ninety and I past fifty, we sat together in her home, as I was about to leave for Europe. This proved to be our last brief visit. We prayed together with clasped hands that day, confident I am sure that "if our earthly house of this tabernacle were dissolved, we have a building of God, a house not made with hands, eternal in the heavens." (1 Corinthians 5:1.)

Then there was "Aunt Roxy" Brock. It was always a glad day to me when she and her husband, Isaac, an elder in the Pleasant Grove Church, came to the store. Their wares were of the best, the eggs were always fresh, their butter the sweetest and most fragrant. Mrs. Rapp reserved these for her select trade, a bon-ton boardinghouse down the road toward Shawneetown. But such things did not intrigue me. Two lovely little girls, twins they seemed to me, were always along. They were of about the same size and always dressed alike. Their brown hair and eyes caught my boyish fancy. I was to see them later, when selling dry goods in the county seat, and later still, but . . .

One Saturday I heard Aunt Roxy say to Mrs. Rapp, "I'd like to get a salt cellar if there's anything left over." Then Mrs. Rapp said to me, "Sammy, get up on the wood box there and get one of those salt cellars we got in yesterday and show it to Mrs. Brock." I made the sale. I had to take my eyes off the little girls standing by the stove, but not for long.

Nine years later I would take the younger of the two from a comfortable farm home to be the wife of a preacher. As we two were leaving for our parish, some two hundred miles away, her mother brought out that salt cellar and gave it to us as a start toward our scant household furnishings. I have it yet and around it clusters the memory of the three good women who meant much to me.

Married at sixteen, Aunt Roxy raised to maturity eight sons and daughters. At the golden wedding all were living and

209

well, with fifty-four grandchildren and sixteen great-grandchildren, not a dim eye, a lame leg or arm, a moral quirk, or a religious freak in the whole lot.

This busy woman had religious convictions enough and of stalwart quality. A denominational journal that disapproved of the use of instruments in worship had a place in her home. She espoused that cause with Spartan zeal. Never once in all my comings and goings in her home, or hers in mine, was that issue mentioned. Once when my young son was starting to Sunday school with his cello, she said to him in my hearing, "What's that thing you've got?" "It's a cello, Grandma, I play it at Sunday school." With a combative overtone she said, "You'd better throw it away and get a New Testament." As we walked to the church on that Sunday morning, he said to me, "Grandma sure has some peculiar ideas; but I guess they are all on the safe side."

However, the years had a softening effect. When I was ministering for a college church, this worthy woman, then at home with us, would start early on Sunday morning to sit in the sanctuary and listen to the half-hour pipe organ prelude of familiar hymn tunes she had heard and sung for years in the old home church. It was not until we had laid her body to rest near Pleasant Grove Church by the side of her beloved Isaac, that her youngest son brought from the county seat the reed organ to support the voices of their numerous descendants as they brought their tribute of praise to the God she loved and sought to serve.

Preachers are said to move a good deal. My Clara knew that when she married me. That is—or was—one bugaboo of the minister's family life. But there are compensations. Not everyone in a community can pull up stakes and leave behind the people he does not like and who do not like him—love them though he ever must. But there is another side to it, as every preacher's wife must know: they retain the large company of

210

faithful folk who have endeared themselves to the family, and add the new and usually larger congregation with whom social and spiritual contact will be made.

Thirteen times we gathered together our household effects to invade a new field of labor. The actual moving was the least of it, though invariably we lost money in the process, since we were never adequately repaid by the slow-growing increase of income. Thirteen times we had to meet and learn to know intimately and work agreeably with these new families. Thirteen times, having taken to our hearts the dear saintly ones to be found in every congregation, we had to bid them good-by and go questing into another community to make new friends. Through it all, Clara stood faithfully, cheerfully, uncomplainingly at my side. Four times, though burdened with the multiplicity of petty engagements required of a mistress of the manse, she went happily to her couch of pain that we might rejoice together with a family of growing sons and daughters. A thousand times or more she suffered without sign of impatience or word of resentment the secret sting of unmeant cruelties inflicted on preachers' wives by the preacher himself when nervous or weary or by parishioners who talk thoughtlessly and too much. In gatherings of women around the quilt or washing dishes at the sink in the church kitchen, when unwise or unsavory speech got going, her unassuming presence, purposely thrust in, would put a sudden stop to it all and raise conversation to higher levels. We often talked of all this at night when we were alone together and of how God had blessed us and how happy we had been together.

Often, when lonely and disconsolate among strangers and far from home, I called by telephone just to hear her voice and be comforted by it. Once, when exiled for too long a season in a Pittsburgh hotel, I recalled that it was October fifth, our wedding anniversary. I immediately sent her a fifty-word night letter as tender and affectionate as I could write. At once came her answer telling me how, on receiving it, she had knelt alone in our living room in Cincinnati to thank God for our long and happy life together and for the children he had given us.

This is too tender and personal to be told in a book. But I would like to tell every young married pair of the gain to be had by simple, frankly spoken appreciation of those we love. It is so easy and so essentially just that those who are companions for life lay aside all reserve and speak freely their deeper feelings. My regret now is that I did not do it oftener.

How quiet was the house when she had gone from me! How desolate life became without the steadying presence I had known so long! I wandered from room to room, caressing the valued books I did not care now to read, sitting hesitant at the typewriter desk, unable to form a worthy sentence. I paused sometimes before her picture to say how I had loved her and to shed a tear, remembering some word of mine, now past recall, that must have hurt. Gradually I came to feel that having had her so long, I had her still and ever would—not the busy and often weary and perplexed housewife she had been, but the clear image in my own conscious inner life of what she had always wished to be.

A day came presently, in that overshadowing loneliness, when my mind would stray back along the paths we had traveled together, to find, if I might, one like her who would share with me the fragment that remained of a busy, burdened life. One long known and loved by both of us came. It was all very strange at first, but, with the passing weeks, came a singular blending of the two faces and life became livable, even radiant again.

One day, in the new relation, as we were returning from service in a rural church, I ventured to soliloquize to her after this fashion: "There is some advantage in being a second wife." "Just what?" she instantly asked. "A man will remember all the mistakes he made in the earlier relation and will try to make up for them in the new." I should have known better than to have said that. She was silent for the moment, then sighed softly and said, "It must be heavenly to be the third." I looked covertly to see if there might be a twinkle in her eye. She had turned her face from me, but I caught the stray ripple of what seemed to be a faint smile that stole round her cheek. In time I learned not to leave an opening like that; for a man, though a preacher, will learn if given time.

These I have known best and loved most. God made woman to be loved, to keep love alive in the hearts of us men who must so often go out into a harsh, corrupt and unfeeling world. It is sad that women are not all and always lovely and lovable. Perhaps if they were loved more, more honestly, more purely, more intelligibly, they would be. There is enough of what love attracts and seeks in each one of us to save and transform. It is, truly and pactically and not only sentimentally, love that lifts; not so much the love of others for us as the love we exercise toward others.

So many women who are good and pure and purposeful have come near me that the mutual outreaching of a love that is not at all of the flesh has given me a measure of emotional balance and poise and kept my face uplifted from the sod. Among these is the wife of Deacon Skelton—diminutive, unassuming, utterly unselfish, always busy with some housewifely care or chasing the last speck of dust from porch or front steps. The steamed pudding she could make, the way she could roast a light Brahma hen in that cast-iron cookstove, the warm hospitality that was almost a compulsion to the young preacher, the motherly friendship during my boyhood ministry; her fervent prayers and tender thoughts followed me all the years, through all the States and across the sea into other lands.

Another was the young widow of my close friend who perished at an early age in the waters of Senatchwine Lake. Courageously she gathered together the loose ends of a growing estate

213

and carried on through the lonely years until their four small children had arrived at honorable maturity well qualified for the exigencies of adult life. On the table in her home, always in view, was a treasured likeness of the one man she had loved, kept there through the dragging decades of her long widowhood. Though young and attractive and what the world calls rich, she loved but once and to the end of her days was loyal to that love.

Then there was Lucy Ferguson who lived in her cottage home on ten acres with Larney, her husband, and their two daughters. Through all their several wanderings, when the girls were grown and the little farm sold, she was the same consecrated, unassuming, uncomplaining soul. In Kansas they helped to establish a new church. In Oklahoma they revived and saved one about to be abandoned. In the slashes of Wisconsin they conducted funerals when no minister was near and she wrote the tribute for Larney to deliver. When left alone, she "went softly all her days," until at the last they brought her body to the quiet spot of her earlier life and laid it to rest among the friends of her youth.

John Buchanan's wife always considered their farmhouse the guest preacher's home. When a cantankerous faction sought to seize old Leatherwood meetinghouse, she walked more than two miles, carrying with her a bucket of drinking water to keep watch for hours and to make sure that the faction did not enter the building until a court decision could be secured. I tasted her gooseberry pie on the fourth Sunday in May, thirty-seven years ago, and have jockeyed round the tables at many an annual gathering of Leatherwood Church since to try to find another delicious triangle of it, for even though she is gone these years, the recipe, and much else besides, she had passed on to the younger women in the church.

"Let your women keep silence in the churches," said Paul (1 Corinthians 14:34); and also, "I suffer not a woman to teach." (1 Timothy 2:12.) Paul was inspired with good sense as well as spiritual guidance during an age of social upheaval. The cautions he gave were essential, even imperative then. But Jesus, and the good news he brought, has made it clear to us that in Christ there is neither male nor female. If women were to keep silence in the churches of today, there would be a distressing silence. They are helpfully vocal everywhere and at all times. When men falter or fall short in spiritual obligations, the women take over and, like Phoebe, "servant of the church at Cenchreae" and friend of Paul, see to it that the powers of the unseen world do not prevail against the church nor the gospel message be hindered in its conquest of mankind.

Chapter 20

Unfinished Business

I am in love with life on this planet of ours. This I dare to say though not unmindful of thistles and thorns, hurricanes and earthquakes, floods and dust storms; to say nothing of the human eccentricities, perversions, and inconsistencies one must endure to live here. I do not wish to give it up now or ever, unless it be for something assuredly better. I have had a good time here.

It would not surprise me if any future existence that may be in store for any part of our race would have its setting right here. God has many places, but why go to any other? Not many changes would be needed. Do away with sin, sickness, death, hospitals, graveyards, and penal institutions and this could be made into a measurably acceptable heaven for a redeemed and perfected race. Some scientists say we are only in the morning of creation. The Scriptures, dealing with our enemies and obstacles, declare that "the last enemy to be overcome is death."

It seems to me to be a fairly well-ordered world as things are. What is that we call Providence? Something real and immeasurable, I am sure. It is a pet surmise of mine, allowing for providence as a necessary hypothesis, that nothing ever just happens. If it were possible to trace out, identify, and correlate all influences, forces, agencies, I believe we would find that there is now one ongoing plan and one life, flowing on like a mighty river, to some shining, shoreless sea, the life eternal. The life of an individual may be but a tiny trickle, an eddy, a bit of drift—as certainly mine has been—but it is a part of the whole just the same, and, as such, entitled to consideration. If fitly told, its story may be well worth the reading.

This writing in semiautobiographical vein, as I have done, is treacherous business. I have felt the peril of it all along. Who sets himself to it had better don a garb of sackcloth, throw ashes on his head, and eat no food for a period of days. To select from remembered incidents only those that are of general significance, to exhibit them dispassionately against a suitable background without show of secret self-esteem, to divulge the deep matters of the heart and not make unnecessary display of personal emotions is a task to be shunned, not sought after.

I have written to confess, not to gratify ambition. I have seen my name in print often enough, in letters large enough, and have suffered keenly enough from having written or spoken out of turn, that I might well hesitate, on the very threshold of another book, to shed sandals and don wading boots lest what seems to be holy ground become but sinking sand. I am glad to be safely through with it.

This is the confession of a self-trained man. It is the story of one who, through no choice or fault of his own, of sheer necessity had to take life in rough-and-tumble fashion and make his observations from unconventional points of view.

Of course, there can be no such thing as a self-made man. Any man has been made, as far as he has been made at all, by such influences as have touched his unfolding life. But also, paradoxical as it may seem, every man worth the while is a self-made man, in that with all the abundance of materials, agencies, and influences, he still has had to be the architect and builder of his own character and destiny.

It is not wholly a misfortune when one is denied easy passage along the customary ways of human improvement and progress. Any handicap, if accepted as a challenge, may prove to be rare and precious capital. Something is to be gained in traversing the detours, unchosen and unwelcome though they always are. Adventure waits at every curve and intersection for him who has eyes to see and ears to hear. There are no road signs but new scenes along the way compensate. There is satisfaction, too, coming back to the highway again, in having seen that which was denied those journeying on main traveled roads.

The detours of life, indeed, offer materials for an eventful story if ever it can be suitably told. Many a notable one has been bounced over these stumps, pulled out of these chuckholes, begrimed by this dust. The Hugh Millers, the Joseph Parkers, the Booker Washingtons, and the David Lloyd Georges are a numerous company, a fellowship of deathless renown with which it is high honor to have had any small experience in common.

It is agreed, I think, by men who have had to do with the selection of efficient aids for difficult work, that there is something to be said for the intelligent amateur. The professionally trained expert knows that there are, let us say, five ways to do a certain thing. He tries them all, and, failing, gives it up. The amateur does not know how many ways there may be and so he keeps on trying—six, ten, twenty—until he stumbles upon a way original with him. Thomas A. Edison tried over seven hundred materials in his quest for the filament used in the incandescent light bulb. The journalist seeking an understudy, is apt to choose a cub reporter who is alert, in preference to the graduate of a school of journalism. Many, if not most, of the great discoveries have been made by amateurs scouting on un-explored frontiers.

In my own case, with all the obligations of the grown-up man laid on me at the age of thirteen, there was the added necessity of getting an education to fit me for one of the learned professions. In pursuit of this treasured ambition I had re-course, as herein told, to rather unusual individual effort, to original research, and to every supposedly helpful artifice within reach, including, of course, close contact with elect souls. I have had to watch from the side lines a good deal of the time, but that is not a bad way to learn the rules of the game. There was always this advantage, not to be had in schools: if I did not like what I was at, or if I thought I could spend my time with greater profit elsewhere, I was free to do so. And I al-ways knew of a dozen other interesting projects I could under-take with profit and satisfaction.

I believe, too, that I have made an interesting discovery. It is parallel to one made by road builders in a certain locality. There was such lack of suitable materials that the improved highways required for motor traffic seemed out of the question. Yet the native clay made travel impossible in winter and un-pleasant because of dust in summer. An experiment was made. Carload lots of material were brought in from distant gravel banks and stone quarries to be distributed in low ridges along the roadside when the ground was hard. Then men with shovels and hand rakes put a thin coating on the track. This was soon ground into the clay, so that a new coating had to be applied. This, too, was ground in, as was another, and an-other; by that process, over several seasons, a far better road was made with one third the material, than is usual where materials were abundant. I am convinced that education may well be acquired by a similar process. The plan followed hitherto, and still, with few exceptions, is to take the boy or girl at six and apply unwelcome education constantly through eight

219

years of grade work, four years of high school and then, perhaps, four more years of college, not to mention university or special professional training. The graduate is fairly stuffed with undigested and untried material.

As a result of this the favored ones, when finally they have finished, often think themselves educated and are glad of it, for they are tired of school. Constant application to book and class work has left them little time to get acquainted with life and the kind of world they are to live in. The material has not been ground into the native clay. So, clothed in cap and gown, thousands come forth each year, many of them well-schooled though often but little educated, unable to get jobs or to hold one when it is secured, to earn money or to save it when it has been earned. These simple, fundamental things they must be able to do if they are to have worthy places in our kind of world. There ought to be such changes as would allow education to be "applied in thin layers," each one to be wrought into character by daily contact with practical life before another is applied. When this is done, even if it be by sheer necessity, men of new and unique type may be produced; men who, without diploma, degree or other academic certification, may be able to render vast service to society. Hitherto men like this have seemed to appear by accident, chance, or providence, but this educational process by force of circumstance may be better in the long run.

Our well-meaning schoolmen have so far expanded curriculums that the dispensable three R's, grammatical technique, and essential history have been well-nigh crowded out as though they were antique relics of some distant and fast-retreating age. This defect began to be seen some thirty years ago when Cincinnati University led out with its combination courses of study and work. More recently Antioch College has been operating such a program by which each student spends a prescribed time during his college years working at some job in business or industry to develop a view "which makes the great concepts of the humanities meaningful and translatable into practical terms." A national magazine has recently publicized the "Presbyterian Institute of Industrial Relations," launched in Pittsburgh and lately removed to Chicago, called "Ministers in Industry" by which industrial plant jobs are prescribed for ministerial students as part of their course of preparation. It would seem that education, the drawing out and developing of individual endowments, is still in process of evolution. Maybe it is as yet unfinished business. I take some pride in the fact that long before any of these innovations were even thought of, I, from downright necessity, was working my way blindly by this as yet unpublicized theory of education. Others in generations long gone had done so with distinction.

Such schooling as this—and it is schooling, whatever may be said of it, though much of the time without book, teacher, or classroom—adds luster to life. The habit of prying into things and learning through personal initiative and the innate desire to know, once it is acquired, is a permanent treasure that will not rust or corrupt and that no thief can break through and steal. Edison, at seventy-three, worked fourteen hours a day on a bowl of soup, a handful of solid food, and with but four hours' sleep. His whispered word, "It is very beautiful over there," as nature brought release and his spirit drifted off in the last dreamless sleep, was a fitting climax and farewell for such a life.

The visible world, really invisible to so many, is always a wonderland to the reverent and inquiring. Every little blossom by the roadside has its interesting history. Every weed of the fields has treasure for him who will but seek it. Every briar-grown hillside, the woodland glen, the mountain steeps, and the ocean deeps invite, beckon, beguile with promise of endless diversion. Science, with book and apparatus, waits each earnest searcher after truth. All nature, the soil below

221

and the sky above, the stately ships of cloud sailing majestically by, invite to rare adventure and enchanting discovery.

The unseen universe, the world of spirit, is, after all, the real and eternally enduring. We have scarcely touched the hem of that garment of our unseen God. Here the simple and unschooled will often excel—"All the fitness he requireth is to feel our need of Him."

All about us, undervalued always because so common as to be unnoticed or so corrupted as to be despised, is our own human kind, chattering, loving, hating, brooding, quarrelling, bargaining, planning, working—each in his own way—the great family to which we all belong. These have interested me most. But for them and their need I might have been content to build a rude dwelling place in some wooded spot by a waterside, and there abide in peace—a companion of the harmless living things that do not reason or worry or speak—there writing, just for the love of it. Indeed, I think I have always been unconsciously peeved at the universe, impatient with life, querulous and disagreeable at times, because I have not been allowed to thus indulge such vagrant fancies. Destiny has seemed to hold me to practical things and my nemesis of haste to keep me going at high speed to the next most needy waiting task. But who of us can be sure that the course in life he was compelled to take was not the best for him? The necessity that compels may be the providence that guides.

Time and life have taught me a thing or two. Any person, busy with a multiplicity of taxing engagements, is apt to look longingly at some other field of endeavor than his own and to imagine he would be happier there. He knows the hurts and handicaps where he is, but looking abroad he sees only the allurements. These are but momentary flights of the mind. They seem to relieve at the moment and to freshen a passing grouch. But happiness—as much of it as we merit—is where we are if only we will look for it and qualify to know it when it meets us face to face.

It was long ago, when browsing through someone's bookcase, that I chanced upon Thoreau's *Walden*. The plan of it, the author's simple style, and the unassuming humility of the narrative gripped and held me. Most compelling of the paragraphs I read and reread was this cryptic passage:

> I long ago lost a hound, a bay horse, and a turtle dove, and am still on their trail. Many are the travellers I have spoken concerning them, describing their tracks and what calls they answered to. I have met one or two who have heard the hound, and the tramp of the horse, and even seen the dove disappear behind a cloud, and they seemed as anxious to recover them as if they had lost them themselves.

Something down deep in me answered instantly to that. I knew what he meant. I read it to half a dozen friends of mine. One or two of them looked thoughtful and asked me to read it again. Others stared and blinked and went away.

It was years later that I found this very passage quoted in John Burroughs' *Literary Values*. The genial naturalist saw in it reference to "A search for the transcendental, the undefinable, the wild that will not be caught." By that time I had joined Thoreau in the quest for his lost possessions and, like his other friends, had found traces of them, had seen the track of his horse, heard the coo of his dove, and the bay of his hound.

But in spite of the lure of the literary I have been interested most of all in people—to know them, to love them, to pity them. The smile of a year-old baby, the cry of an older child, the silent agony of parents suffering from that hidden pain that is sharper than a serpent's tooth—these have seemed to me to be treasure hidden in a field, the place of service most insistently and irresistibly calling; and "for joy thereof" I have gladly given up all else to buy that field.

Many have seemed to be in dire need of what I, and only I, was willing to do for them. The best blessings of my life, perhaps of any life when lived out satisfactorily, have been those stern commanding duties that keep me from frittering away time with inconsequential matters, from using precious days to amass money that may never be needed or to attain to cheap distinction, valued only by mediocre minds.

I have never lived in "a house by the side of the road," enchanting as that simile may be when one is shut up in a city apartment or dozing by a winter fire. I have passed many such, though, and have sometimes lingered briefly for a chat with them. Strangely enough, as has happened, the one who greeted me and bade me enter, sometimes seemed to know me and to be awaiting my arrival. One inquired why I was so long in coming; others have generously urged that I stay on or asked where I was going and why I was in so great a hurry. A select few have joined me (and Thoreau) in our quest for the unattainable.

So much to see, so much to learn, so much to suffer or enjoy! And but one brief human life for it all! How long the unfinished journey! How short the day! I shall never have done with life, I know. It is an unfinished business.

Excuse me, please—I must run along now.